THE USBORNE NATURE TRAIL BOOK

CONTENTS

Malcolm Hart, Ingrid Selberg, Margaret Stephens,
Su Swallow, Sue Tarsky, Ruth Thomson

Consultant editors: Peter Holden, Sally Heathcote, Chris Humphries, Alfred Leutscher BSc, Jean Mellanby,
E. H. M. Harris, Michael Chinery, Denis Owen, Alwyne Wheeler, Anthony Wootton
Additional advice from Peter Holden, Chris Humphries and Alfred Leutscher

Designed by Amanda Barlow, Sally Burrough, Nick Eddison, Niki Overy, Diane Thistlethwaite, Robert Walster
Design revision by Non Figg, Julia Rheam, Diane Thistlewaite, Robert Walster and Kathy Ward

Edited by Bridget Gibbs, Helen Gilks, Sue Jacquemier, Ingrid Selberg
Editorial revision by Rachael Swann

Bluetit

Nuthatch

If you are walking along a
seashore, rambling in the
countryside or sitting in a
city garden, you can always
find birds. This section of
the book will help you to
identify them and give you
lots of information about
their habits.

When you go bird
spotting take this book
with you and turn to the
pages which deal with the
kind of place you are
visiting, such as a wood or
pond. Pages 28-31 will give
you extra help by showing
you the size of certain
birds.

The birds on these pages are not
drawn to scale

Chaffinch

BIRDWATCHING

Contents

Siskin

Stonechat

How to be a birdwatcher

The most important thing to have when you go birdwatching is a notebook. If you try and keep all the facts in your head, you will probably forget some of the important ones.

Make sure any notes you make are clear and readable. The picture on the right shows how to set your notebook out. Try to draw the birds you see. Even a bad drawing is better than no drawing at all.

Notes on shape, size, colour and flight pattern will be important later, if you need to identify a bird.

A birdwatcher has to take notes quickly. Use a spiralbound notebook, like the one here. It has a stiff back to help you write easily. File your notes away in date order when you get home or write them up into a neat book. When you are out, put your notebook in a plastic bag to keep it dry.

Look carefully for the shape and obvious marks first. The male Reed Bunting here has a sparrow-like body and beak, a dark head, white collar and white outer tail feathers. It also has a dark throat and dark flecks on its side.

Male Reed Bunting

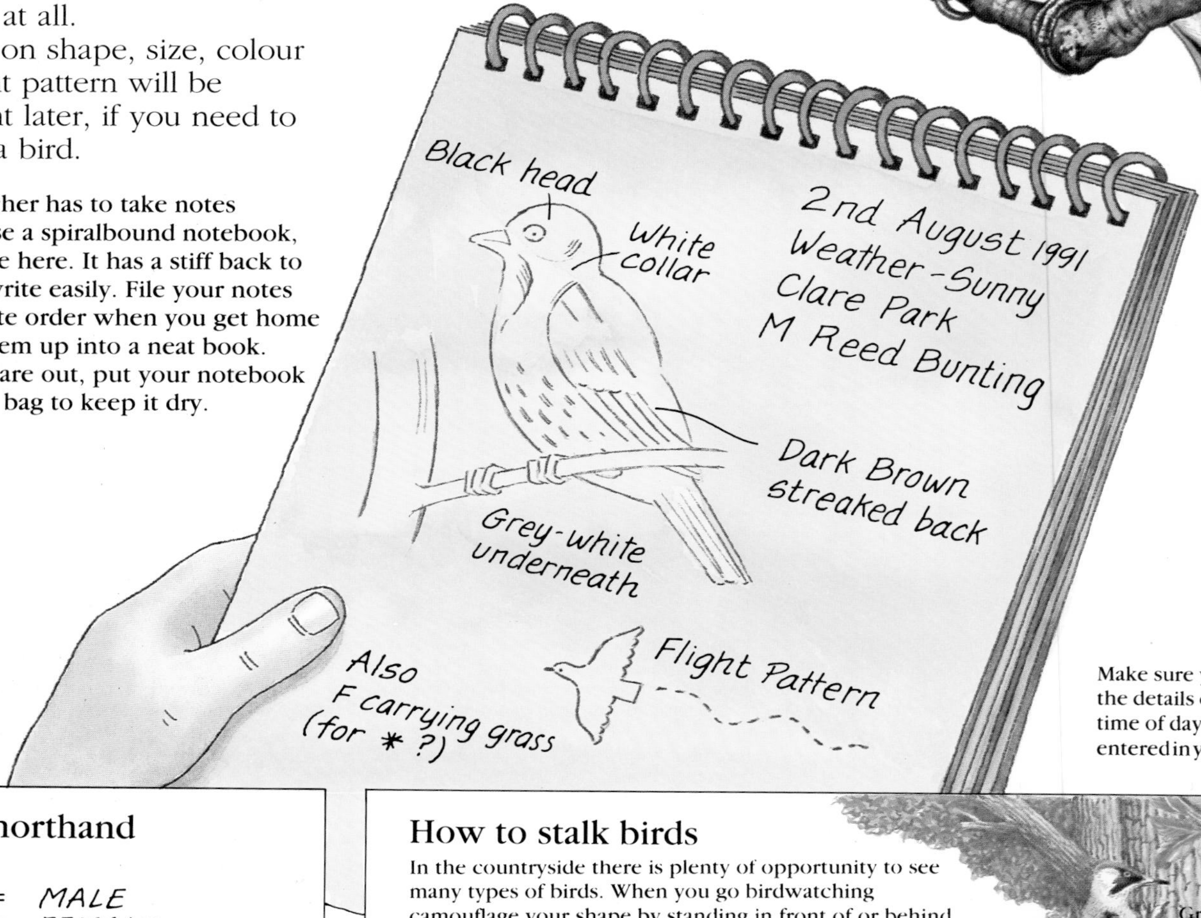

Black head

White collar

Grey-white underneath

2nd August 1991
Weather - Sunny
Clare Park
M Reed Bunting

Dark Brown streaked back

Also
F carrying grass
(for * ?)

Flight Pattern

Make sure you have all the details of place, date, time of day and weather entered in your notebook.

Bird shorthand

M = MALE
F = FEMALE
JUV = JUVENILE (YOUNG BIRD NOT IN ADULT FEATHERS)
* = NEST
C10 = ABOUT TEN (WHEN TALKING ABOUT NUMBERS OF BIRDS)

Use these signs instead of writing out the words. It will save you time. Always take two pens or pencils with you.

How to stalk birds

In the countryside there is plenty of opportunity to see many types of birds. When you go birdwatching camouflage your shape by standing in front of or behind a tree or bush. Keep the sun behind you, so you are in shadow. If there is no cover, crawl closer using your elbows and feet. Don't wear clothes that rustle when you move. Never move quickly in the open.

Green Woodpecker

Willow Warbler

Woodcock

What to wear

Travel as light as possible. Remember to wear dull colours.

Anorak or warm coat.

Hat or hood.

Wellingtons if wet. Trainers at all other times.

Notebook and pencils.

Buying binoculars

Choose the lightest pair you can find. The best size to get is 8 x 30 8 x 40.

Binocular strap

Belt

String tied to strap and belt.

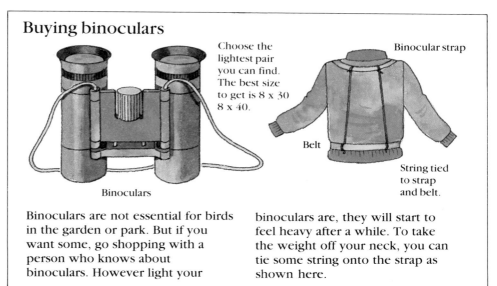

Binoculars

Binoculars are not essential for birds in the garden or park. But if you want some, go shopping with a person who knows about binoculars. However light your binoculars are, they will start to feel heavy after a while. To take the weight off your neck, you can tie some string onto the strap as shown here.

Quick field sketches

1 Two circles for head and body.

2 Add beak, neck, tail and legs.

3 Add details of feathers.

The best way to make notes on the birds you see is to draw quick sketches of them. Begin by drawing two circles - one for the body and one for the head.

Notice the size and position of the head and body before you start. Add the tail, beak, legs and then add details of feathers if you have time. Do not draw what you do not see. Practise by drawing the birds you can see from your window or sit on a bench in the park and draw the birds there.

Remember to use your ears as well as your eyes. Birdsong is very important when you go birdwatching. It is often the first clue to tell you that a bird is near. The Jay, pictured here, has a very raucous call . Other sounds can give you clues too. You will often hear a Green Woodpecker drilling a hole in a tree before you see it.

You will not get far loaded with heavy equipment and you will be unable to move easily and quietly. If birds can see your shape silhouetted against the sky, they will fly off.

Chaffinch

Nuthatch

Jay

Chaffinch

How water birds feed

Swallow catching insects over the water.

Pintail up-ending.

Kingfisher diving for fish.

Wigeon grazing on land.

Moorhen feeding in reeds by the water.

Grey Heron fishing on the edge of the pond.

Mallard dabbling on the surface.

Mute Swan fishing with head and neck under water.

Tufted Duck diving.

Watch how different kinds of birds feed on your local pond. Which birds up-end the most? Which dabble the most? Which dive the most? Why is it do you think that some kinds feed differently from others?

Taking off and landing

Goldeneye

Most water birds are heavy and must work hard to get up speed for their take-off. Many of them run over the surface, flapping their wings until they are going fast enough to become airborne. Coming in to land, they fly low over the water, with their feet sticking out. These act as a brake when they touch down on the surface.

Gull

Moulting

Mallards moult in late summer. The male loses his colourful feathers and becomes a mottled brown all over. For a time he looks rather like the female. New bright-coloured feathers grow by early winter.

When danger threatens Mallard ducklings, the mother stretches out her neck and quacks loudly. The ducklings dive to escape.

Woodlands and forests

Woodlands and forests are good places to spot birds, but you will see them more easily in places that are not too dark. Woods with open spaces are lighter and have more plants and insects for birds to eat.

Woods with broad-leaved trees, such as oak and beech, contain many more birds than old pine forests, which can be very dark. But old pine forests can have special birds, such as Capercaillies, that can be found nowhere else.

The **Goldcrest** (9 cm) is the smallest European bird. It is often found in coniferous or mixed woods all year round.

The **Nightingale** (16.5 cm) can often be heard singing in woods and forests, but is rarely seen. It builds its nest among trees and bushes close to the ground.

The **Coal Tit** (11.5 cm) is the same size as a Blue Tit. It nests in coniferous forests.

The **Chaffinch** (15 cm) is a common bird, often found in broad-leaved woodlands and coniferous woods. In winter it prefers to live in open land.

The sizes given are beak-to-tail measurements.

If it is windy, watch out for falling branches in the woods. Try not to stand or sit near trees which have nests in them. You might frighten away the parent birds.

The **Chiffchaff** (11 cm) is smaller than a sparrow and visits Europe from Africa during the summer. It is often found in broad-leaved woods and in young pine plantations.

The food of woodland birds

The Tawny Owl feeds on small animals. Its eyesight and hearing are very good.

In autumn, Jays collect acorns. They bury many of them and then dig them up when they need food.

Many birds, such as the Garden Warbler here, feed on caterpillars.

The Pied Fly Catcher swoops down on insects from a look-out branch.

Jay

Special beaks

Some birds, such as the Hawfinch and the Crossbill, have special beaks for eating seeds.

Hawfinch

Crossbill

The **Black Woodpecker** (46 cm) is the largest European woodpecker. It is found mainly in coniferous forests in many parts of Europe, but not in Britain.

Holes in trees

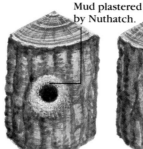

Mud plastered by Nuthatch.

Hole used by a Nuthatch.

Hole used by a woodpecker.

Woodpecker holes

4 cm Lesser Spotted

4.5 cm Great Spotted

6.5 cm Green

10 cm Black

The different kinds of woodpecker all make nesting holes in trees. These are sometimes used by other birds, such as the Nuthatch, or even bats and dormice.

The **Nuthatch** (14 cm) feeds on nuts from hazel, beech and oak trees.

The **Green Woodpecker** (32 cm) is the same size as a pigeon. It is frequently seen on the ground, feeding on ants, and is usually found in broad-leaved woodlands.

The **Woodcock** (34 cm) is found in broad-leaved woodlands where its plumage blends in perfectly with the dead leaves on the ground. It has a long, thin beak.

The **Lesser Spotted Woodpecker** (14.5 cm) is the smallest European woodpecker. It is found in broad-leaved woods. The male bird has a bright red crown.

Woodlands at night

There are many different kinds of owl living in woods. They range in size from the small Pygmy Owl, which is only 16.5 cm high, to the much bigger Eagle Owl, which can be as large as 71 cm.

These four owls are all drawn to the same scale.

These three owls are all drawn to the same scale.

The Nightjar sleeps during the day, so is rarely seen. Its song can be heard after dark in summer.

Pygmy Owl

Scops Owl **Little Owl**

Little Owl

Long-eared Owl

Tawny Owl

Eagle Owl

Nightjar

Towns and cities

Bird spotting in towns and cities can be just as rewarding as in the countryside. In densely built up areas, you may only see Pigeons, Starlings and House Sparrows. Where there are gardens and parks you will find many other kinds of birds.

Some of these birds are quite used to people and can be very tame. You may even be able to get quite close to them and tempt them to feed from your hand. The pictures here show some of the most common birds in towns and cities.

The **Kestrel** is a town as well as a country bird. The town Kestrel usually feeds on sparrows, and nests high up on the tops of buildings.

Cliff birds that live in towns

Black Redstart

Black Redstarts once nested on sea-cliffs and rocks. Now you are more likely to find them in towns. They make their nests on buildings.

The **Long-tailed Tit** is a hedge bird that can often be seen in parks and gardens. In autumn and winter, family groups of about a dozen gather together.

The **Black-headed Gull** is one of the commonest town gulls. You will often see large numbers of them near reservoirs and gravel pits and in large grassy areas.

You will never see a **Swift** on the ground or on a wire. It feeds and even sleeps on the wing. At dusk, Swifts circle high above the roof-tops.

You will sometimes hear the warbling song of the **Skylark** as it flies above parks and wasteland. In winter, you may see flocks around gravel pits and reservoirs.

1
Towns and cities are surprisingly good places to look for birds. Birds need food and a place to rest and sleep. Most gardens (3) and parks (2) have

2
some trees and bushes where birds can nest and sleep without being disturbed by people. Many birds find perching places on buildings (5). Gulls fly out to

3
sleep at gravel pits (1) or reservoirs (4). Everywhere people spill or leave food which birds can eat. On the edge of town, birds find lots of food at sewage

Rock Dove

Pigeons

The town Pigeon is a relation of the Rock Dove, which nests on sea-cliffs. The town Pigeon is now much more common than the Rock Dove and is often very tame. It feeds on bread and any other scraps it finds in parks or in the streets, and can be a nuisance in city centres.

Noisy city birds

Starling

Starlings are one of the most common city birds. They are usually found in huge, noisy flocks.

House Martins build their mud nests under the roofs of many town houses.

Carrion Crows are quite common in parks and gardens.

Magpies are large black and white birds and are common in parks and gardens. They use twigs to build their nests in tress and tall hedges.

White patch only on House Martin.

Swallows look rather like House Martins, but have longer tail feathers. You can often see them catching flies over rivers, gravel pits and reservoirs.

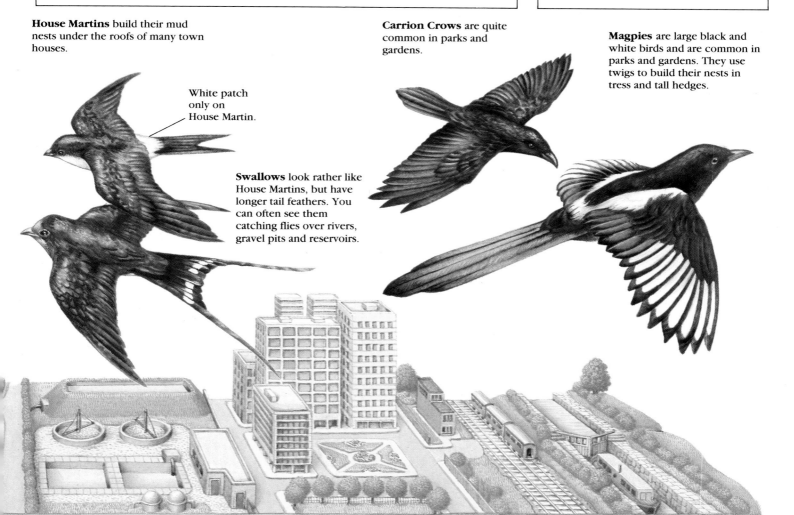

4
works (4) and rubbish dumps (1). Railway sidings and canals (6), where food supplies are unloaded and often spilt, are also good feeding spots for

5
birds, and have fewer people to disturb them. Many birds eat the seeds of weeds growing on waste ground and building sites. In winter, when there is

6
little food in the countryside, many birds fly to the towns and cities. There many people put out food specially for the birds.

Jackdaw. 33 cm. Has a grey head and is smaller than the all-black crows.

Magpie. 46 cm. A large bird with a long tail and black and white plumage.

Carrion

Hooded

The northern form of the **Carrion Crow** (47 cm) has some grey feathers. It is called the **Hooded Crow** (47 cm).

Rook. 46 cm. Has a thinner beak than the crow, with a bare white face and "baggy trousers".

Curlew. 51-58 cm. Largest wader. Has a long downward curved beak, a brown body and long legs.

Pheasant. Male 66-89 cm. Female 53-63 cm. A large gamebird. The male is brightly coloured, the female browner with a shorter tail.

Male

Female

Large water birds

These birds are NOT drawn to the same scale.

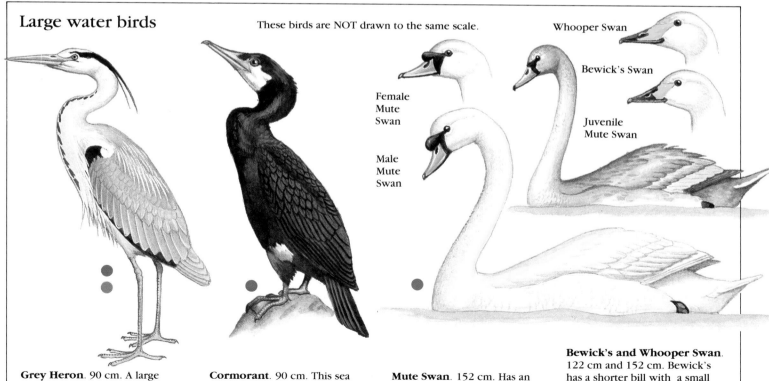

Whooper Swan

Bewick's Swan

Juvenile Mute Swan

Female Mute Swan

Male Mute Swan

Grey Heron. 90 cm. A large grey bird, often seen standing at the water's edge. The nest is usually built in a tree.

Cormorant. 90 cm. This sea bird has a white chin and cheeks. Often seen sitting on rocks with its wings half open.

Mute Swan. 152 cm. Has an orange bill with a black knob at the base. Swims with its neck curved.

Bewick's and Whooper Swan. 122 cm and 152 cm. Bewick's has a shorter bill with a small yellow patch. Both hold their necks stiffly when swimming. They are winter visitors.

Birds in flight

Here are some illustrations to help you identify birds in flight. The sizes given are beak-to-tail measurements.

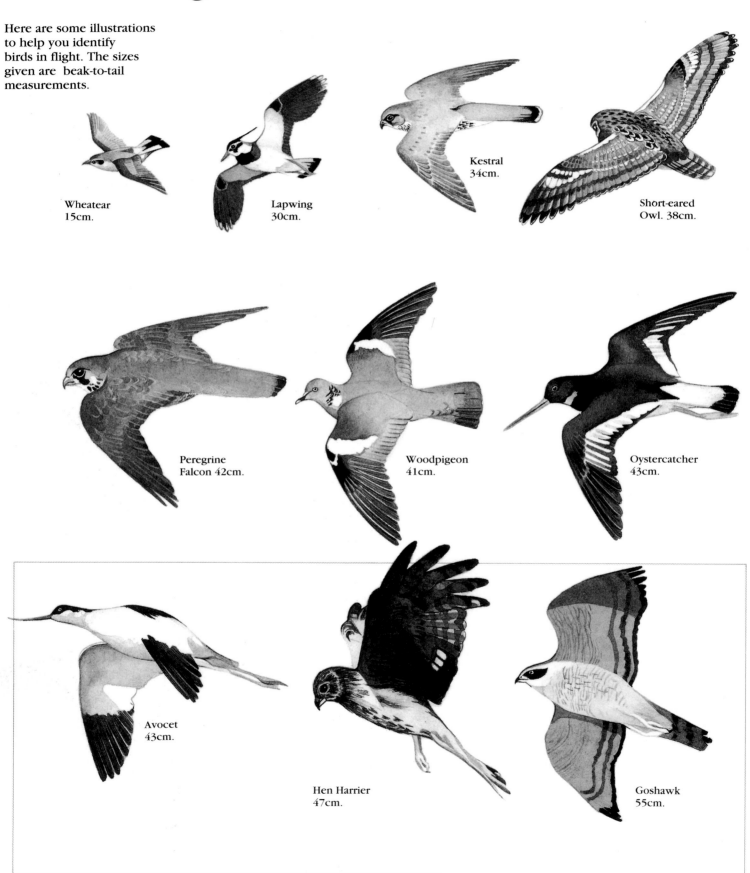

Wheatear
15cm.

Lapwing
30cm.

Kestral
34cm.

Short-eared
Owl. 38cm.

Peregrine
Falcon 42cm.

Woodpigeon
41cm.

Oystercatcher
43cm.

Avocet
43cm.

Hen Harrier
47cm.

Goshawk
55cm.

Buzzard
54cm.

Osprey
54cm.

Black Kite
54cm.

Herring Gull
60cm.

Mallard
58cm.

White-tailed
Eagle 69-91cm.

Greylag goose
76-89.

White Stork
102cm.

Pheasant
66-89.

Mute Swan
152cm.

33

Trees are everywhere. Only deserts and the tops of mountains are without them. This part of the book tells you about trees and how to study them. It shows you the different parts of a tree, how they work and how they can help you to identify the tree.

It tells the whole story of a tree, from the moment a seed sprouts to when a mature tree dies or is cut down for timber. There are also special tips on how to collect information and specimens.

If you want to identify a tree, look first at pages 60 to 63, called *Common trees you can spot*. If you fail to find a picture of your tree there, turn to the pages that deal with the part of the tree you are looking at, such as a leaf or a piece of the bark.

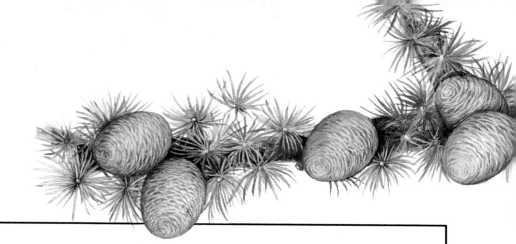

TREES & LEAVES

Contents

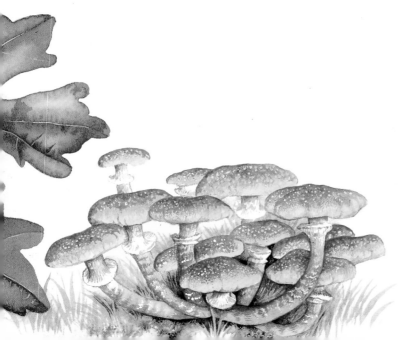

How a tree grows

This is the life story of a Sycamore, but all trees grow in a similar way. Although there are many different kinds of trees, they all sprout from seeds, grow larger, have flowers, form fruits and shed seeds.

You can study many of these steps in a tree's life. You can watch a tiny seedling sprout and then keep a record of its growth. You can count the girdle scars on a young tree to find out its age.

Older trees have flowers and fruits, although they may be hard to see on some trees. Not all trees have flowers as large as the Horse Chestnut's or fruits as big as the Apple tree's. Most fruits ripen in autumn, but some appear in early summer and spring.

An important part of a tree that you do not usually see is the roots. If you find an overturned tree, look at the roots and try to measure them. Look also at logs and tree stumps for the layers of wood and bark. They can tell you the age of the tree and how quickly it has grown.

The tree starts growing in spring from a seed which has been lying in the soil all winter. At this time, with the help of the food stored inside it, the seed sends down a root into the soil to suck up water and minerals.

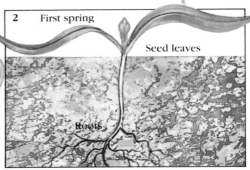

Next, the seed sends up a tiny shoot which pokes above the ground and into the light. Two fleshy seed leaves open up with a small bud between them. These leaves are not the same shape as the tree's real leaves will be.

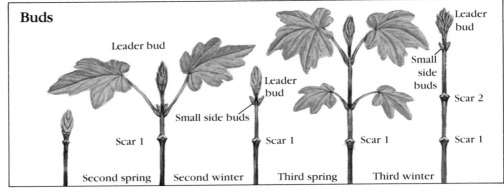

In the second spring, the bud opens and there are two new leaves. A new shoot grows too, with another bud at the tip. In autumn, the leaves drop off. Every year the same thing happens, and every time the leaves fall off, they leave a girdle scar on the stem. Buds on the sides of the stem also grow shoots, but they do not grow as fast as the leader shoot at the top of the tree. Each year the tree grows taller, and the roots grow deeper.

Pollen on the flowers

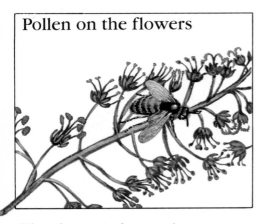

When the tree is about twelve years old, it grows flowers on its branches in the spring. Bees and other insects, searching for nectar, visit the flowers and some of the pollen from the flowers sticks on to their hairy bodies.

Fruits

When the bees visit other flowers from the same tree, some of the pollen on their bodies rubs off on to the female parts of the flowers. When the pollen and female parts are joined, the flowers are fertilized and become fruits.

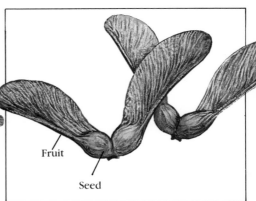

Later that year, the fruits fall off the tree. The Sycamore fruits here spin like tiny helicopters, carrying the seeds away from the parent tree. The wings rot on the ground, and the seeds are ready to grow the following spring.

3 Leaves

Seed leaves

First summer

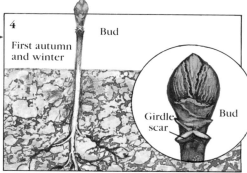

4

First autumn and winter

Bud

Girdle scar

Bud

Holly leaf

The seed leaves have stored food in them to help the seedling grow. Soon the bud opens, and the first pair of real leaves appears. These will trap light from the sun to grow more food. The seed leaves then drop off. The roots grow longer.

In the autumn, all the leaves change colour and drop off, leaving a "girdle scar" around the stem where they were attached. A bud is left at the end of the shoot. The bud does not grow during the winter. It stays dorment.

Many broadleaved trees are deciduous, which means that they lose their leaves in autumn. They do this because their leaves cannot work properly in cold weather, and there is not enough sunlight in winter for the leaves to make food for the tree.

Most conifers are evergreens. Their needles are tougher than most broadleaves, and they can keep making food even in the dark of winter.

A few broadleaved trees, such as Holly, are also evergreen. Like conifer needles, their leaves have a waxy coating which helps them survive the winter.

Inside a tree

Each year, a tree grows more branches. The trunk thickens by adding a new layer of wood to hold the branches up, and the roots grow deeper and wider. This picture shows you the inside of the trunk, and all its different parts.

1 Heartwood. This is old sapwood which is dead and has become very hard. It makes the tree strong and rigid.

2 Rays. In a cross-section of a log you can see pale lines. These are called rays and they carry food sideways.

3 Cambium. This layer is so thin that you can hardly see it. Its job is to make a new layer of sapwood (see page 20) each year. This makes the trunk thicker and stronger.

4 Sapwood. This layer also has tiny tubes in it which carry the sap (water and minerals) to all parts of the tree from the roots. Each year a new ring of this wood is made by the cambium.

5 Phloem. Just inside the bark are tubes which carry food down from the leaves to all parts of the tree, including the roots.

6 Bark is the outer layer which protects the tree from sun, rain and fungi which might attack it.

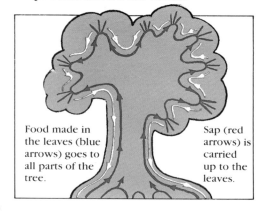

Food made in the leaves (blue arrows) goes to all parts of the tree.

Sap (red arrows) is carried up to the leaves.

To help it grow, the tree makes food for itself in the leaves, which contain a green chemical called chlorophyll. In sunlight, the chlorophyll can change oxygen from the air, water, and minerals brought up from the soil into food for the tree. If a tree gets no light to make food it will die.

Scots Pine cone

Seeds fall out of cone.

Some trees, such as the Scots Pine, have fruits called cones, which stay on the tree, but open up to let the seeds fall out by themselves. When the cones are old and dried up, they usually fall off the tree too.

How to identify trees

One of the best ways of identifying a tree is to look at its leaves. Be careful though, because some trees have leaves that are very similar. For example, a London Plane leaf could be confused with a Norway Maple leaf. So when you have named your tree just by identifying a leaf, always check that you are correct by looking at other parts of the tree, such as the flowers or bark.

Trees can be divided into three groups: broadleaved, coniferous, and palm trees (see the pictures to the right here). Try to decide which group your tree belongs to. There is something to give you clues in every season of the year. In spring and summer, look at the leaves and flowers. In autumn, look at the fruits. Winter is the best time to study buds, twigs, bark and tree shapes.

You do not need to go into a woodland or forest to study trees. Look at the many different kinds that grow in gardens, parks and roads. Sometimes you can find rare trees in gardens.

Broadleaved trees

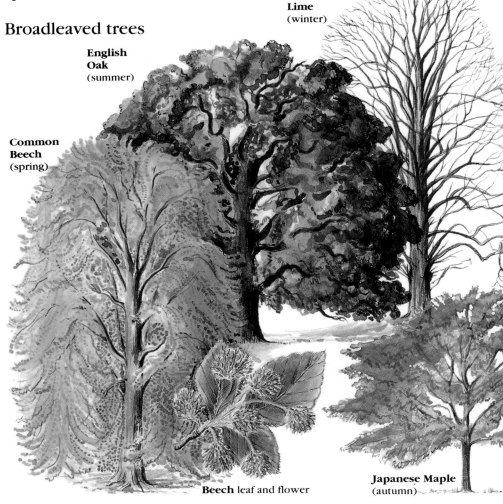

Lime (winter)

English Oak (summer)

Common Beech (spring)

Beech leaf and flower

Japanese Maple (autumn)

Most broadleaved trees have wide, flat leaves which they drop in winter. Some broadleaved trees, though, such as Holly, Laurel, Holm Oak and Box, are evergreen and keep their leaves in winter.

Broadleaved trees have seeds that are encased in fruits. The timber of broadleaved trees is called hardwood, because it is usually harder than the wood of most conifers, or softwood trees.

Tree or shrub?

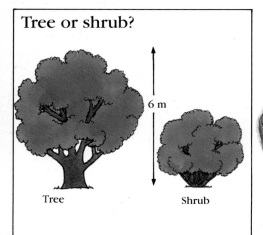

6 m

Tree

Shrub

Trees are plants that can grow to over 6 m high on a woody stem. Shrubs are smaller, and have several stems. See page 59 for how to measure trees.

What to look for

Leaves

Yew (conifer)

Common Beech (broardleaf)

Oak (broadleaf)

The leaves will give you the biggest clue to the identity of the tree, but look at other parts of the tree as well. There is a guide to leaves on page 40.

Shape and bark

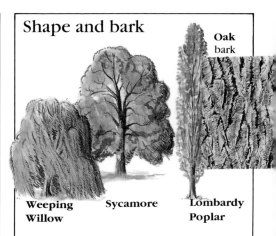

Oak bark

Weeping Willow

Sycamore

Lombardy Poplar

The overall shape of the tree and its crown is also a good clue (see page 44). Some trees can be identified just by looking at their bark.

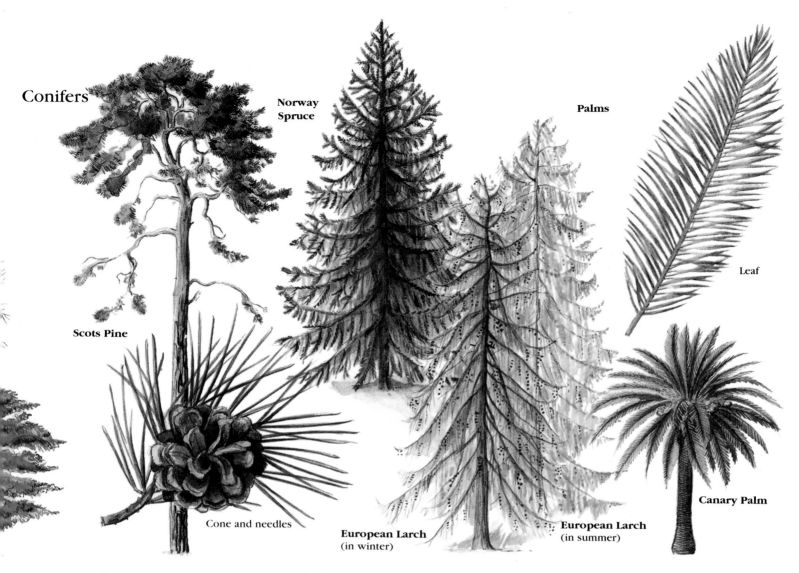

Conifers

Scots Pine

Cone and needles

Norway Spruce

European Larch (in winter)

European Larch (in summer)

Palms

Leaf

Canary Palm

Most conifers have narrow, needle-like or scaly leaves, and are evergreen, that is they keep their leaves in winter. The Larch is one conifer that is not evergreen, as the tree loses its leaves in winter.

Conifer fruits are usually woody cones, but some conifers, such as the Yew, have berry-like fruits. The overall shape of conifers is more regular and symmetrical than the shape of most broadleaved trees.

Palms have trunks that have no branches. They look like giant stalks. The leaves grow from the top of the tree. Unlike other trees, palms grows taller without getting thicker.

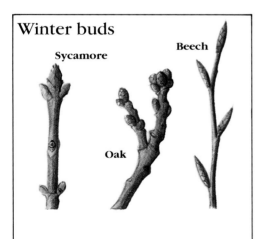

Winter buds

Sycamore

Beech

Oak

In winter, when there are often no leaves to look at, you can identify some trees from their buds, bark and shape. See page 43 for bud shapes.

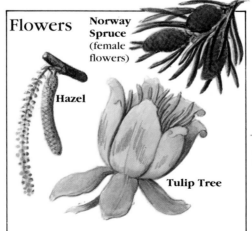

Flowers

Norway Spruce (female flowers)

Hazel

Tulip Tree

In certain seasons a tree's flowers can help you to identify it. But some trees do not flower every year. For tree flowers, see pages 46-47.

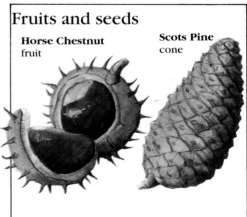

Fruits and seeds

Horse Chestnut fruit

Scots Pine cone

All trees have fruits bearing seeds which may grow into new trees. This Horse Chestnut conker and the pine cone are both fruits. See pages 48-49.

Leaves

One of the things that most people notice about a tree is its leaves. A big Oak tree has more than 250,000 leaves and a conifer tree may have many millions of needles.

The leaves fan out to catch as much sunlight as possible. With the green chlorophyll inside them, they make food for the tree. They take in gases from the air through tiny holes, and give out water vapour and gases in the same way. Once the food is made, it is carried through veins to other parts of the leaf. The veins make the leaf strong like a skeleton.

The leaf stem carries water from the twig and also helps the leaf to move into the light. It is tough so that the leaf does not break off in strong winds.

The leaves of broadleaved trees and conifers look different, but they do the same work. Most conifer leaves can survive the winter, but the leaves of most broadleaves fall off in the autumn. A conifer needle stays on a tree for about three to five years.

Tracking down your mystery leaf

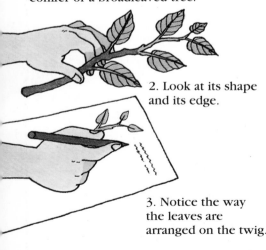

1. Decide if the leaf is from a conifer or a broadleaved tree.

2. Look at its shape and its edge.

3. Notice the way the leaves are arranged on the twig.

4. Look at the colour and leaf surface.

Conifer Leaves

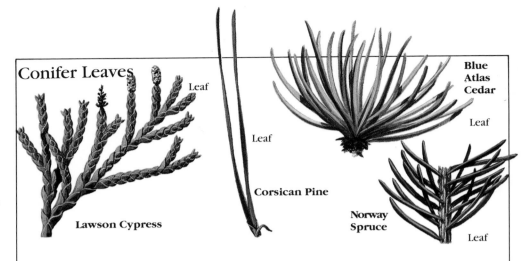

Leaf

Leaf

Corsican Pine

Lawson Cypress

Blue Atlas Cedar

Leaf

Norway Spruce

Leaf

Here you can see three types of conifer leaf. Many conifers have narrow needle-like leaves which are either single, in small bunches or in clusters. They can be very sharp and spiky. But other conifers, such as the Cypresses, have tiny scale-like leaves, overlapping one another.

Broadleaves
Simple

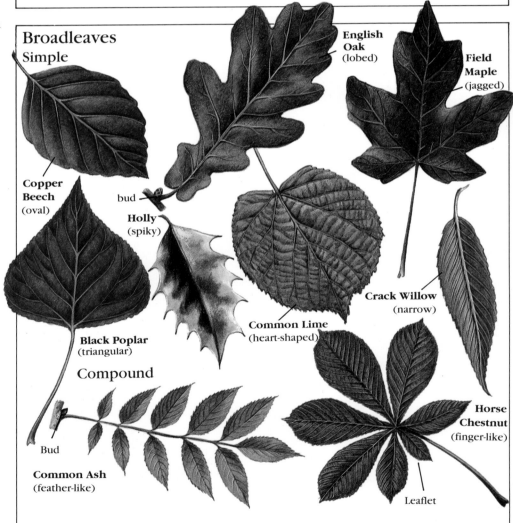

English Oak (lobed)

Field Maple (jagged)

Copper Beech (oval)

bud

Holly (spiky)

Crack Willow (narrow)

Black Poplar (triangular)

Common Lime (heart-shaped)

Compound

Common Ash (feather-like)

Bud

Horse Chestnut (finger-like)

Leaflet

The leaves of broadleaved trees have many different shapes. Leaves in one piece are called simple. Those made up of many leaflets, such as Common Ash and Horse Chestnut shown here, are called compound. Simple leaves and compound leaves both have one bud at the base of their stems.

These leaves are not drawn to the same scale.

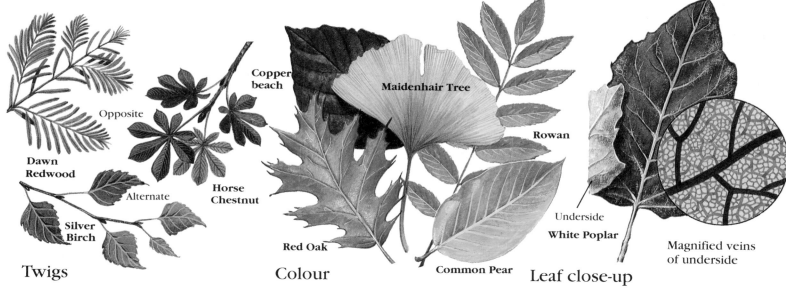

Twigs

Leaves are arranged on twigs in various ways. They can be opposite each other in pairs, or they can be single and alternate from one side of the twig to the other.

Colour

Leaves are green because of the chlorophyll inside them. In autumn, the chlorophyll in broadleaves decays. They change colour before they fall.

Leaf close-up

Leaves have a network of tiny veins. Their upper surface is tough and often glossy, to stop the sun from drying them out. The underside is often hairy.

Leaf scrapbook

Keep a scrapbook of the leaves you find. Place each leaf between two sheets of blotting paper. Then put a book and a heavy object on top.

Leave them for about a week. When the leaves are flat and dry, mount them in a scrapbook with sticky tape. Label the leaves and write down where and

when you found them. When a dead leaf has crumbled, the strong stem and veins remain as a skeleton. You will often find these in winter.

Leaf tiles

Press the leaf on to the "clay" with a rolling pin.

The finished tile can be painted or varnished.

Make your clay by mixing together:
2 cups flour (not self-raising)
1 cup salt
1 cup water
2 tablespoons cooking oil

Scatter some flour onto a surface top and shape your "clay" into a ball. Roll it out flat with a floured rolling pin, until it is about 2 cm thick. Press your leaf, vein side down, onto the clay so that it

leaves a mark. Remove the leaf and bake the clay in the oven at 150°C (250°F) for about two hours. When the tile has cooled, you can paint it or varnish it.

Forestry

Trees have been growing on Earth for about 350 million years. Much land was once covered by natural forests, but they have been cut down for timber and cleared. New forests are often planted to replace the trees that have been cut down.

Because conifers grow faster than broadleaved trees and produce straight timber, they are preferred for wood production.

On this page you can read about the story of a Douglas Fir plantation, and what the foresters do to care for the trees.

Seedbeds

The seeds are sown in seedbeds. When the seedlings are 15-20 cm high, they are planted in rows in another bed where they have more room. They are weeded regularly.

Planting out

When the seedlings are about 50 cm high, they are planted out in the forest ground, which has been cleared and ploughed. There are about 2,500 trees per hectare.

Fire towers on hills help to spot fire - the forest's worst enemy. Fires can be started by a carelessly dropped match or an unguarded campfire.

Plantations can be sprayed with weedkillers and fertilizers from the air.

When the trees are felled, they are taken away to sawmills to be cut up.

Every few years the weaker trees are weeded out to give more light and room to the stronger ones. These thinnings are used for poles or are made into paper.

Trees are felled when they are fully grown (about 70 years for conifers and 150 years for Oaks). About one in every ten trees reaches its full growth.

Dead and lower branches are cut off trees. This lessens the risk of fire and stops knots from forming in the wood.

Wood

The wood inside different types of trees varies in colour and pattern, just as the bark varies. Different kinds of wood are suited for certain uses. Wood from conifers, called softwood, is mainly used for building and making paper. Wood from broadleaved trees, called hardwood, is used to make furniture.

At the sawmill, the person operating the saw decides the best way to cut each log. A log can be made into many different sizes of planks, as well as into paper pulp.

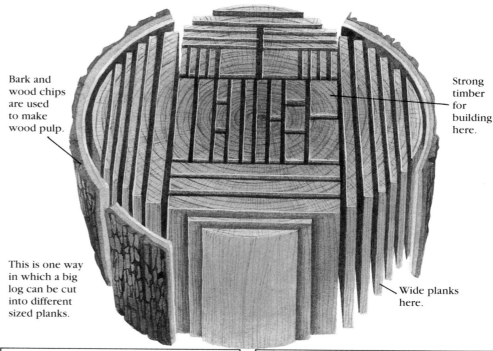

Bark and wood chips are used to make wood pulp.

Strong timber for building here.

This is one way in which a big log can be cut into different sized planks.

Wide planks here.

Grain

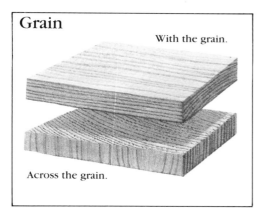

With the grain.

Across the grain.

When a plank is cut from a log, the annual rings make vertical lines which may be wavy or straight. This pattern is called the grain. Wood cut with the grain is stronger than wood cut across the grain..

Knots

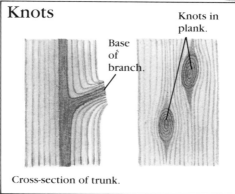

Knots in plank.

Base of branch.

Cross-section of trunk.

In a plank you may notice dark spots, called knots. This is where the base of a branch was buried in the trunk of the tree. This distorts and colours the grain, and so leaves a knot.

Seasoning

Air gets in between the timber.

Fresh wood contains water which is why green logs spit in the fire. As wood dries, it shrinks and often cracks or warps. Planks must be dried out, or seasoned, before they can be used.

Processed wood

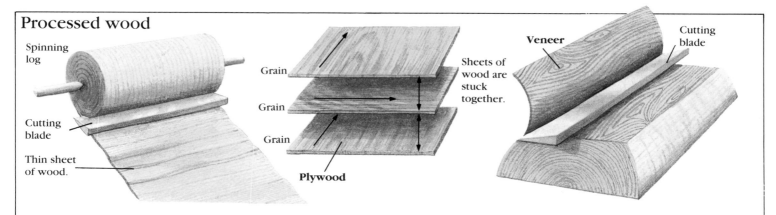

Spinning log

Cutting blade

Thin sheet of wood.

Grain

Grain

Grain

Plywood

Sheets of wood are stuck together.

Veneer

Cutting blade

Much of the wood that you see around you has been "processed". Plywood is thin layers of wood which are glued together with the grain lying in different directions. It is stronger than ordinary wood and does not warp. The thin sheet of wood is peeled off the log like a Swiss roll. Veneer is a thin sheet of wood with a beautiful grain which is used on the surface of plain furniture. Chipboard (not shown) is made of small chips and shavings mixed with glue.

Pests and fungi

Trees are attacked by insects and diseases caused by fungi. Insects use trees for food and shelter, and as places to breed. They can cause serious damage to trees, but they rarely kill them.

Fungi are a group of plants which do not flower. Mushrooms are fungi. Because fungi cannot make their own food, they may feed off plants and animals, and sometimes kill them. Fungi spread by releasing microscopic spores, like seeds, into the tree. These spores can spread and rot the tree.

Leaves and shoots

Spangle galls

Cherry galls

Pine Looper

Gall Wasp

Kidney galls

Green Tortrix

Pine Sawfly

The **Tent Caterpillar** lives in a "tent", which it spins among the branches.

Many moth and butterfly caterpillars and other larvae eat leaves. Often each species only feeds on a certain type of tree.

Oak apple galls

Some insects lay their eggs in leaves or shoots. The tree forms swellings, called galls, around the eggs. The larvae feed inside the galls.

"Pineapple" gall

An **Aphid** made this "pineapple" gall by piercing a shoot to suck out the sap.

Aphid

Leaf Roller

Leaf Miner

Leaf **Miners** eat tunnels through leaves. **Leaf Rollers** fold leaves over themselves for protection.

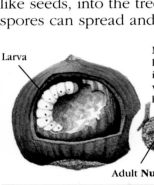

Larva

Nut Weevils lay their eggs inside nuts, where the larvae grow.

Adult **Nut Weevil**

Bark and wood

Conifer Heart Rot is caused by this bracket fungus. It attacks conifers and rots the inside of trees until they die.

White Pine Blister Rust is a fungus which causes swellings on pine trunks and branches.

Look for **Scale** insects on bark. If you pull one off, you may see the grub which sucks sap from the tree.

Elm Bark Beetles make tunnels under Elm bark. They spread the fungus which causes Dutch Elm Disease.

Honey Fungus attacks the roots of many trees. In autumn, their toadstools appear at the base of infected trees.

The **Pine Weevil** strips the bark off newly planted conifers.

Roots

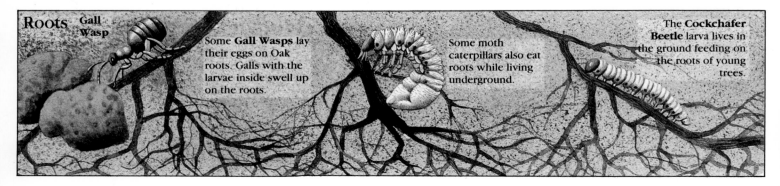

Gall Wasp

Some **Gall Wasps** lay their eggs on Oak roots. Galls with the larvae inside swell up on the roots.

Some moth caterpillars also eat roots while living underground.

The **Cockchafer Beetle** larva lives in the ground feeding on the roots of young trees.

Keeping an Oak apple gall

Netting top tied on with string.

Release **Wasp** when it emerges.

Oak Apple

In summer, collect Oak apples and other galls which do not have holes in them. Keep them in a jar with netting on top. The wasps living inside the galls should emerge in a month.

Making spore prints

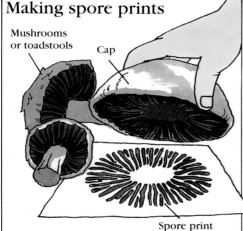

Mushrooms or toadstools

Cap

Spore print

Try using coloured paper too.

Make spore prints from mushrooms. Cut off the stalk and place the cap on some paper. Leave it overnight. It will release its spores on the paper, leaving a print. Always wash your hands after handling a fungus.

Injuries

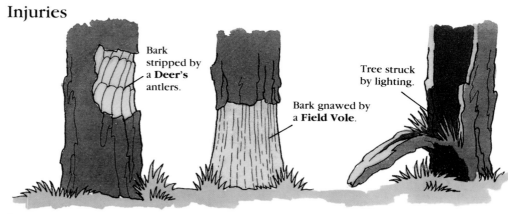

Bark stripped by a **Deer's** antlers.

Bark gnawed by a **Field Vole**.

Tree struck by lighting.

Sometimes trees are damaged by animals. Deer strip the bark off trees when they scrape the "velvet" off their antlers. Squirrels, voles and rabbits eat young bark, which can kill young saplings. If lightning strikes a tree, the trunk often cracks. This happens because the sap gets so hot that it becomes steam. It expands and then explodes, shattering the tree.

How a tree heals itself

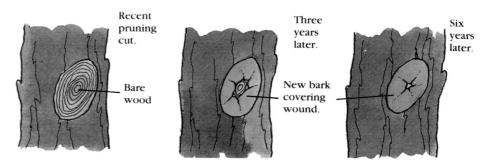

Recent pruning cut.

Bare wood

Three years later.

New bark covering wound.

Six years later.

If a branch is pruned off a tree properly, the wound usually heals. A new rim of bark grows from the cambium around the cut. This finished seal will keep out fungi and diseases. It takes years for a wound to heal. But if a wound completely surrounds the trunk, the tree will die because its food supply is cut off. This can happen when animals strip off the bark.

How trees die

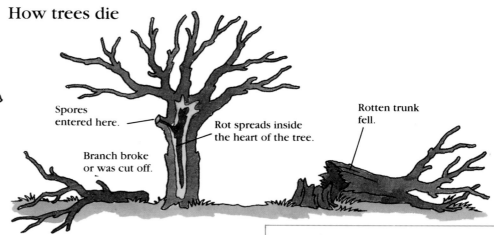

Spores entered here.

Rot spreads inside the heart of the tree.

Branch broke or was cut off.

Rotten trunk fell.

Fungus kills many trees. Spores in the air enter an opening and spread through the tree. The heartwood rots until the tree dies and falls down.

Remember! Never carve your initials or anything else on a tree. It looks ugly and can leave an opening for fungi to enter.

Woodland life

The forest is home to many plants and animals. Trees protect wildlife from bad weather, wind and too much sun. Fallen leaves and twigs make a rich soil called humus. This helps plants to grow. The wildlife in broadleaved and coniferous forests is not the same, although it may overlap.

Trees change carbon dioxide into oxygen. Chopping down trees leaves too much carbon dioxide in the atmosphere which is bad for our planet, making it warmer. This is called the "greenhouse" effect.

A coniferous forest

A coniferous forest is dark and dense. Few plants grow on the ground because of the thick layer of needles and the lack of light. Here are some animals and plants you might see in a coniferous forest.

Pine Marten

Squirrel's drey

Long-eared Owl's nest

Great Spotted Woodpecker

Long-eared Owl

Red Deer

Crossbill

Bracken

Black Grouse

Fox

Norway spruce cones

Wood Ant-hill

Broad Buckler Fern

Timberman

Goldcrest

Fly Agaric

Treecreeper

Lichen

Red Squirrel

Black Slug

A broadleaved forest

A broadleaved forest is more light and open and so attracts many more plants and animals. There are many flowers in spring before the trees' leaves have blocked out the light. As you can see, an Oak wood supports many different kinds of wildlife.

Tree roots help to hold the soil firm. If forests are cut down and the land cleared, the soil can become very loose and dry. This is called erosion.

Mistletoe

Nuthatch

Green Woodpecker

Rook in nest

Tawny Owl

Long-eared Bat in tree

Poor Man's Beefsteak

Blue Tit

Oak

Wood Anemone

Roe Deer

Rabbit

Badger

Bluebells

Pheasant

Ivy

Common Shrew

Hedgehog

Primrose

Moss
Common Toad

Earthworm

Greater Stag Beetle

Speckled Wood Butterfly

Making a tree survey

You will gather many interesting facts about trees and the wildlife they shelter by doing a tree survey. Start with a small area and choose one that has many trees of different types. A piece of countryside, a park, garden or street will all do.

With a friend, make a rough map of your area and add any landmarks, such as roads or buildings. Try to work out a scale for your map - 2 cm for every 50 paces is a good one. Plot each tree on your map and be careful not to miss any.

What to take

Notebook

Tree field guide

Tape measure

Pencils

String

Identifying a tree

Try to identify the trees using this book or another guide. Remember that there are many clues to help you identify them. One type of clue, such as a leaf, is not enough.

Making a map

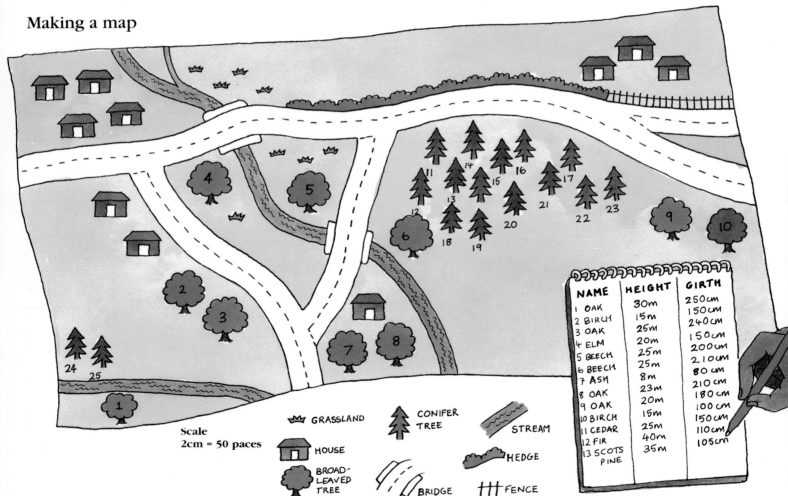

Scale
2cm = 50 paces

GRASSLAND

HOUSE

BROAD-LEAVED TREE

CONIFER TREE

BRIDGE

STREAM

HEDGE

FENCE

NAME	HEIGHT	GIRTH
1 OAK	30m	250cm
2 BIRCH	15m	150cm
3 OAK	25m	240cm
4 ELM	20m	150cm
5 BEECH	25m	200cm
6 BEECH	25m	210cm
7 ASH	8m	80cm
8 OAK	23m	210cm
9 OAK	20m	180cm
10 BIRCH	15m	100cm
11 CEDAR	25m	150cm
12 FIR	40m	110cm
13 SCOTS PINE	35m	105cm

After you have identified and measured the trees (as shown on these pages), make a neater and more detailed copy of your map. Show the scale of your map. Then make a key of the symbols you used, like the one above.

Write down the findings of your survey. Give the name, height and girth of each tree. Repeat the survey later to see if there are any new trees, or if anything else has changed. If you enjoyed making the survey, you can write to the Tree Council * to find out how to do a more complicated one.

Rare flowers

The three flowers shown on the right are very rare indeed. If you think you may have found a rare flower, do not pick it. If you do, the flower will become even more rare and it may disappear completely from the spot where you found it.

Instead, make a careful drawing of the flower and record in your notebook exactly where you found it. Show these to an adult who knows about rare flowers. If it is rare, you can report it to a conservation or nature club.

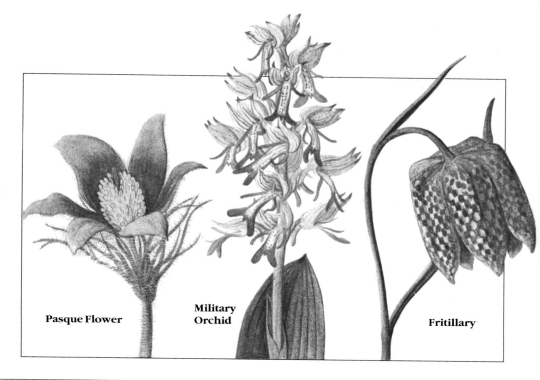

Pasque Flower

Military Orchid

Fritillary

How to make a flower map

The easiest way to make a map is to draw it as you walk along a route you know well. Draw lines for a road or path and make them turn in the same way you do.

Put in symbols for bridges, buildings and other special places. Wherever you find wild flowers, mark the place with a star. Use different colour stars for different types of flowers. Draw the symbols on the bottom of your map and write down next to them what they mean, so that everyone can understand them.

If you like, you can use a scale to show distance. Then anyone looking at it can understand how far apart everything is.

You can choose any scale you want. This map has a scale of 2 cm for every 50 paces.

SYMBOLS FOR YOUR MAP

 FLOWERS

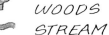 WOODS

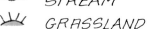 STREAM

 GRASSLAND

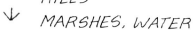 HILLS

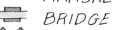 MARSHES, WATER

BRIDGE

HOUSES

How plants live

The Rosebay Willowherb and the Field Buttercup have flowers with petals and sepals. They also have leaves, stems and roots. Most other plants have the same parts, but they can be different shapes and sizes.

Each part of a plant does one special thing that helps the plant to live. Leaves make food for a plant. During the day, they take in a gas from the air called carbon dioxide. This gas, the green colouring in the leaves, water and sunlight are used by the leaves to make food.

Leaves breathe out gases and water and take in gases from the air through tiny holes, so small you cannot see them with a magnifying glass.

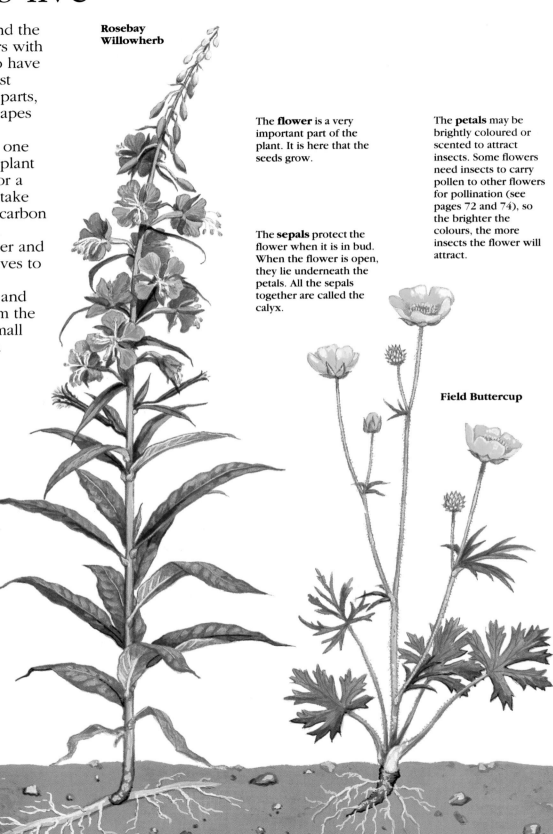

Rosebay Willowherb

Field Buttercup

The **flower** is a very important part of the plant. It is here that the seeds grow.

The **sepals** protect the flower when it is in bud. When the flower is open, they lie underneath the petals. All the sepals together are called the calyx.

The **petals** may be brightly coloured or scented to attract insects. Some flowers need insects to carry pollen to other flowers for pollination (see pages 72 and 74), so the brighter the colours, the more insects the flower will attract.

The **leaves** make food and "breathe" for the plant. They also get rid of any water that the plant does not need. Because leaves need light to make food, the whole plant grows towards light. Some plants close their leaves at night.

The **stem** carries water from the roots to the leaves, and carries food made in the leaves to the rest of the plant. It also holds the leaves up to the light.

The **roots** hold the plant firmly in the ground and draw up water from the soil that the plant needs.

How to identify flowers

Colour and place

When trying to identify a flower the first thing you notice is colour. The shape of its petals, sepals and leaves and the place where you found it are useful also.

Columbine
The Columbine has a blue or dark violet colour. The flower grows in open woods and lowlands.

Bloody Cranesbill
The flowers are a bright purplish crimson and grow in dry, grassy places.

Bluebell
Bluebells are usually blue, but can sometimes be white. They grow in woods and in many grassy areas.

Flowers and stems

One flower on one stem

Small flowers in bunches

Primrose **Cow Parsley**

Plants can have one flower on one stem, or many small flowers bunched together.

Petals

Scarlet Pimpernel **Foxglove**

Petals joined together

Petals separate

A flower's petals may not all be the same shape and size, and they can be joined together or separate.

Sepals

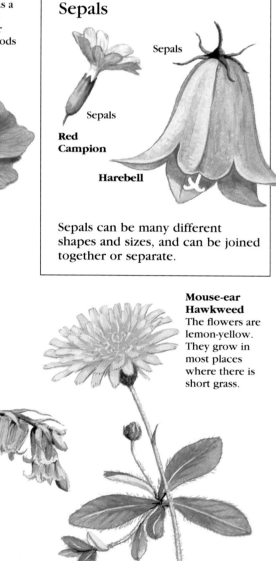

Sepals

Sepals

Red Campion

Harebell

Sepals can be many different shapes and sizes, and can be joined together or separate.

Mouse-ear Hawkweed
The flowers are lemon-yellow. They grow in most places where there is short grass.

Leaves

Wood Anemone

Leaf divides into three parts, joined at the base.

Leaves can be single, as in the Bugle (below). They can also be in separate parts. The Wood Anemone (above) has leaves which divide into three parts joined at the base. Sometimes the parts are on little stalks. These are called leaflets.

Leaflet

Single leaf

Bugle

71

How flowers grow

Almost every plant has a male part, called the stamen, and a female part, called the pistil. The Common Poppy has a group of stamens in the centre of the flower which grow around the pistil (see picture 3).

These pages tell you how the stamens and the pistil in a poppy work together to make seeds and how insects, such as bees, play a very important part by carrying pollen from flower to flower. These seeds will leave the plant and become new plants. Not all plants make seeds in this way, but many do.

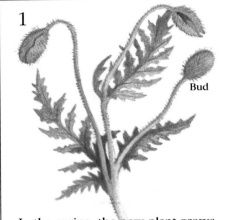

1

Bud

In the spring, the new plant grows from a seed buried in the ground. Later, many buds will develop on the plant.

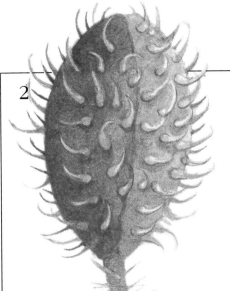

2

The sepals protect the flower when it is inside the bud. As the flower grows, the sepals begin to open.

6 When a bee visits another poppy some of this pollen may fall off onto the other flower's stigma. This is called pollination.

When the pollen grains land on top of the stigma, very thin tubes begin to grow down towards the ovary.

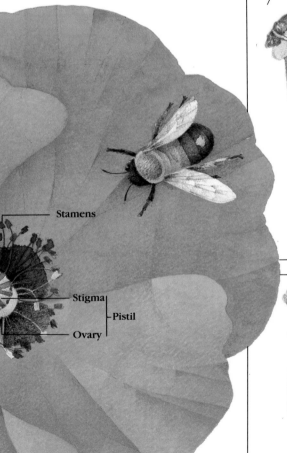

Stamens

Stigma

Pistil

Ovary

The **pistil** has two parts, the **stigma** and the **ovary**. The stigma is the top part. The ovary is the bottom part and holds "eggs", called ovules.

7

Pollen tube

Ovules

Ovary

The tubes eventually reach the ovules in the ovary. The contents of each pollen grain empty into an ovule. This is called fertilization.

11

Holes

The fruit ripens. Its outside walls dry up and holes appear at the top.

72

Shingle Beaches

Not many plants can grow here. These beaches are made of pebbles that once were part of cliffs or rocks. The pebbles have been worn down by the pounding of the sea. There is some sand mixed in with the pebbles, and in many places the shingle is constantly on the move. Only plants with deep roots, such as the Yellow Horned Poppy and the Sea Pea, can anchor themselves firmly enough to survive in the shingle.

Cliffs

Plants struggle to grow here. The winds can be very fierce and blow a lot of the time. Small plants whose roots are not deep can be torn up. The rainwater drains away very quickly, leaving little for the plants. There is almost no soil. Plants must send their roots deep into cracks in the rock. Sometimes they grow along the steep sides of a cliff and can be sprayed with salty water from the sea.

Cliffs may have more soil at the top and there you may be able to find some land plants. Be careful when you look at flowers there. Do not climb any cliffs, and keep well back from the edge.

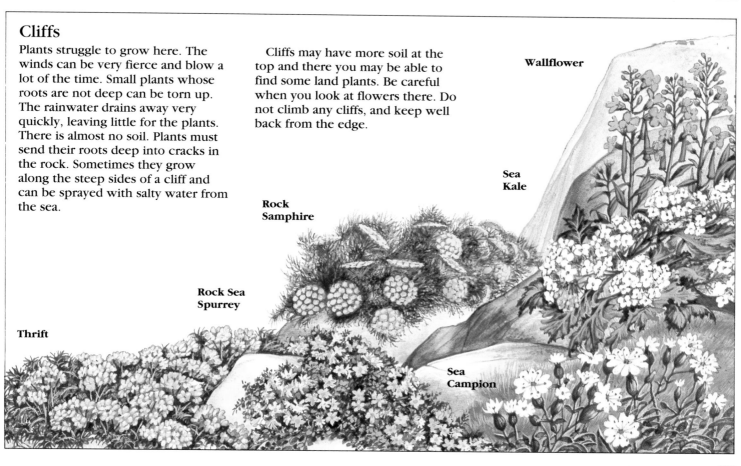

Cities and towns

Flowers grow in waste lands, streets, car parks, gardens, on walls, or any other place in towns and cities where they can find enough soil.

Many flowers can spread quickly over open ground. Some of these flowers are called weeds. Weeds are often stronger than the plants people grow in their gardens, and they can take over. This is a big problem for gardeners.

The flowers in this section are not drawn to scale.

Seed experiment

Heat some soil in an old pan in the oven for about an hour. This will kill any seeds in the soil. Put the pan outside. After a while do wild flowers start to grow? If so, how do you think they get there?

Wallflower
This is a garden flower, but it often "escapes" and can survive from year to year in the wild.

Pellitory of the Wall
This plant looks rather like a Stinging Nettle, but it has no stinging hairs. The stem is reddish-brown.

Ivy-leaved Toadflax
The plant is delicate and trailing, with tiny purple flowers, which have curved spurs. The stems are weak.

Prickly Sow Thistle
The leaves are spiny and clasp the stem. The flowers are pale yellow, about 2.5 cm across.

Dandelion
There is one flower head, made up of many tiny flowers, on each hollow stalk, which contains a milky juice.

Shepherd's Purse
A common weed in cities and towns. The seeds are held in a heart-shaped fruit. Flowers are white.

Ribwort Plantain
The flowers grow on small dark brown spikes. The anthers are pale yellow or purple.

White Clover
The leaves have three (and very rarely four) leaflets. The white flowers have a sweet smell to attract insects.

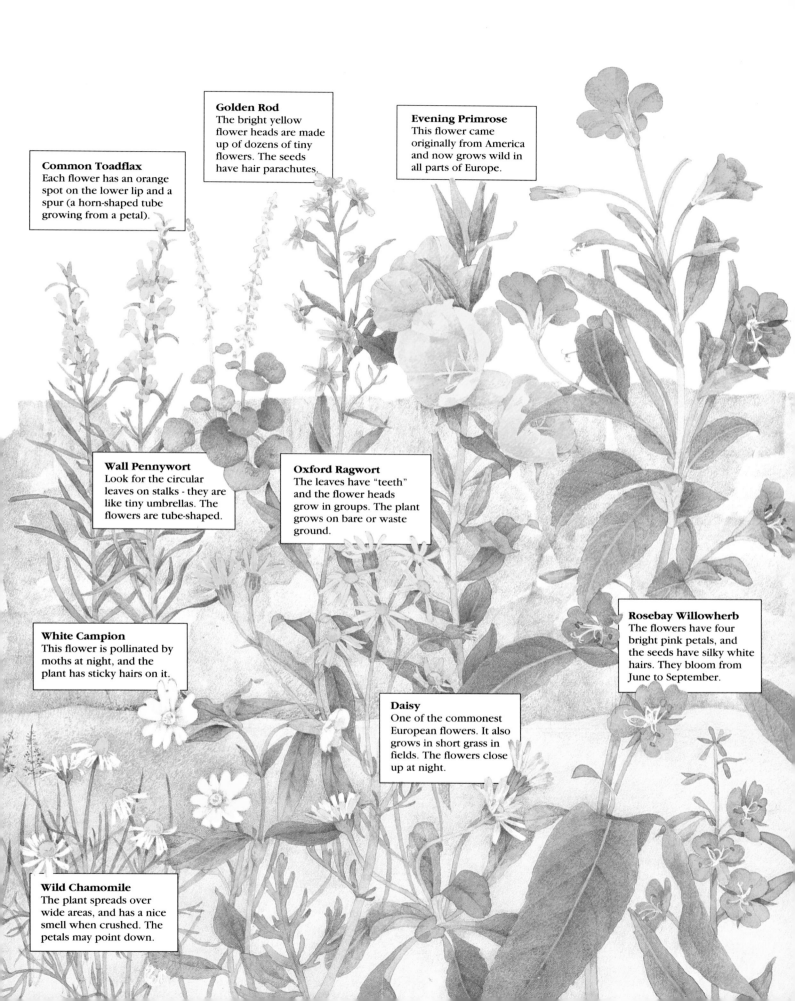

Common Toadflax
Each flower has an orange spot on the lower lip and a spur (a horn-shaped tube growing from a petal).

Golden Rod
The bright yellow flower heads are made up of dozens of tiny flowers. The seeds have hair parachutes.

Evening Primrose
This flower came originally from America and now grows wild in all parts of Europe.

Wall Pennywort
Look for the circular leaves on stalks - they are like tiny umbrellas. The flowers are tube-shaped.

Oxford Ragwort
The leaves have "teeth" and the flower heads grow in groups. The plant grows on bare or waste ground.

Rosebay Willowherb
The flowers have four bright pink petals, and the seeds have silky white hairs. They bloom from June to September.

White Campion
This flower is pollinated by moths at night, and the plant has sticky hairs on it.

Daisy
One of the commonest European flowers. It also grows in short grass in fields. The flowers close up at night.

Wild Chamomile
The plant spreads over wide areas, and has a nice smell when crushed. The petals may point down.

Moors and mountains

Moors

Moors are open lands that are swept by wind. Heathland is very similar. Some of these areas are very dry and some are waterlogged from time to time. Water collects in poor soil, such as in high land or near the coast. You will find fewer flowers on moors and heaths than in meadows and fields. The ones that do grow sometimes take over large sections of land.

Different flowers grow on different types of moors and heaths. The most common moorland plant is Common Heather. Sometimes it is burnt to encourage new shoots to grow. The Common Gorse is very widespread on heaths.

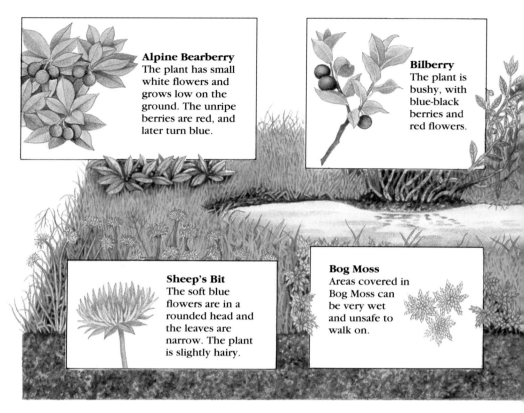

Alpine Bearberry
The plant has small white flowers and grows low on the ground. The unripe berries are red, and later turn blue.

Bilberry
The plant is bushy, with blue-black berries and red flowers.

Sheep's Bit
The soft blue flowers are in a rounded head and the leaves are narrow. The plant is slightly hairy.

Bog Moss
Areas covered in Bog Moss can be very wet and unsafe to walk on.

Mountains

The seeds of mountain flowers find it difficult to grow in the poor soils and the cold, windy weather of mountains. The higher up a mountain you go, the fewer flowers you will find. Trees cannot grow high up on a mountain because of the strong winds and lack of soil.

Some plants can grow high up on a mountain-side. They grow low so that the strong winds will not blow them away. Many mountain flowers spread by sending out creeping stems, which root.

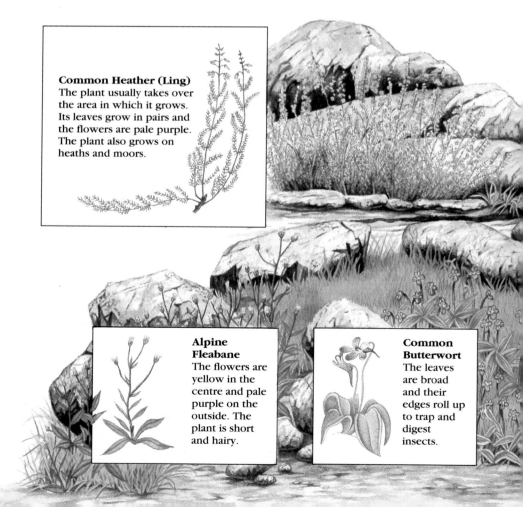

Common Heather (Ling)
The plant usually takes over the area in which it grows. Its leaves grow in pairs and the flowers are pale purple. The plant also grows on heaths and moors.

Alpine Fleabane
The flowers are yellow in the centre and pale purple on the outside. The plant is short and hairy.

Common Butterwort
The leaves are broad and their edges roll up to trap and digest insects.

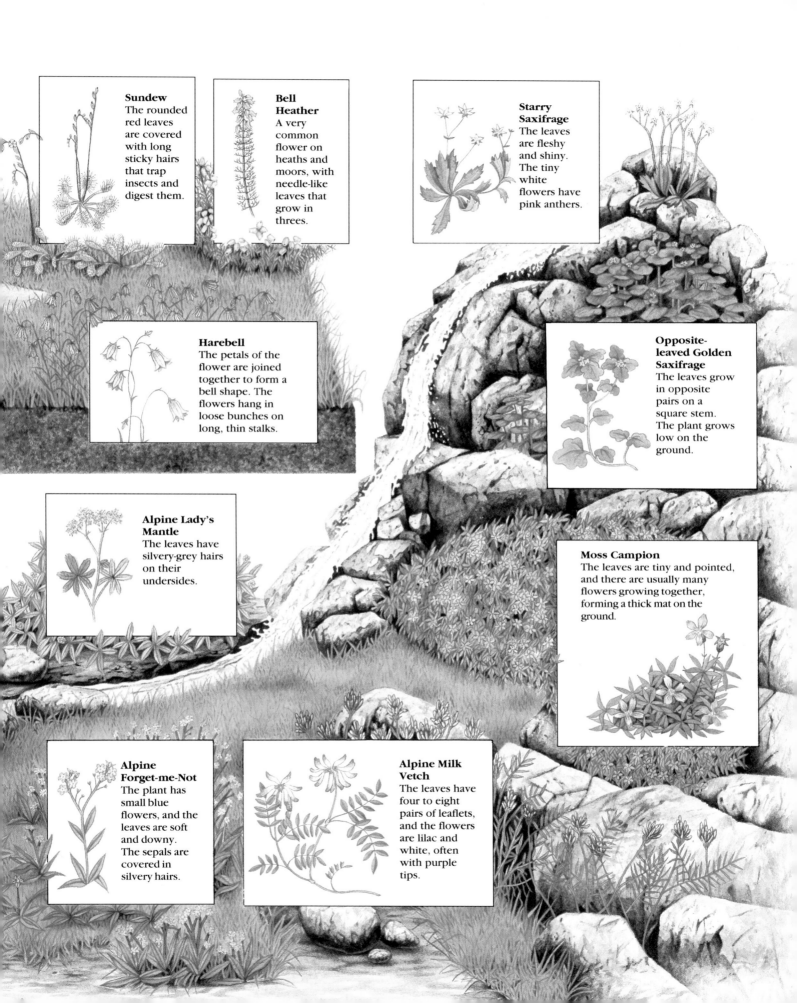

Sundew
The rounded red leaves are covered with long sticky hairs that trap insects and digest them.

Bell Heather
A very common flower on heaths and moors, with needle-like leaves that grow in threes.

Starry Saxifrage
The leaves are fleshy and shiny. The tiny white flowers have pink anthers.

Harebell
The petals of the flower are joined together to form a bell shape. The flowers hang in loose bunches on long, thin stalks.

Opposite-leaved Golden Saxifrage
The leaves grow in opposite pairs on a square stem. The plant grows low on the ground.

Alpine Lady's Mantle
The leaves have silvery-grey hairs on their undersides.

Moss Campion
The leaves are tiny and pointed, and there are usually many flowers growing together, forming a thick mat on the ground.

Alpine Forget-me-Not
The plant has small blue flowers, and the leaves are soft and downy. The sepals are covered in silvery hairs.

Alpine Milk Vetch
The leaves have four to eight pairs of leaflets, and the flowers are lilac and white, often with purple tips.

Shrubs hide insects such as the Speckled Bush-cricket. Hedgehogs may hibernate in leaves under hedges.

Speckled Bush-cricket

Hedgehog

Rotting compost heaps hide many small animals. Look for worms, beetles, millipedes, centipedes, and harvestmen.

Centipede

Brandling Earthworm

In winter, look in corners of garden sheds for spiders and hibernating ladybirds. You may find a Wood Mouse in a shed.

Two-spot Ladybird

Spider

Wood Mouse

Bees and butterflies visit flowers to feed on nectar.

Bumble Bee

Orange-tip Butterfly

Look under logs and stones, and in other damp, dark places for animals like this woodlouse.

Woodlouse

Flower borders provide shelter for snails, caterpillars and slugs.

Dot Moth caterpillar

Brown-lipped Snail

Blackbird

101

Life in the soil

The soil in your garden is full of small animals, although many can be too tiny to see. Different kinds of animals and plants need different types of soil. Snails, for example, need lime in the soil for making their shells. Moles will visit your garden only if the soil is soft enough for them to dig in.

You will be able to find some of the garden animals shown on these pages, by digging in the soil. Some animals, such as earthworms, help to keep the soil healthy, but other animals can damage plants by feeding on the roots and shoots.

Making a wormery

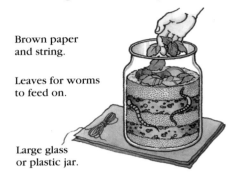

Brown paper and string.

Leaves for worms to feed on.

Large glass or plastic jar.

Put alternate layers of fine sand and soil in a large jar. Then put in a few worms and some leaves for them to feed on. Wrap paper round the jar to keep the light out. Remove the paper two days later and you will see how the worms have mixed up the layers.

Looking at soil

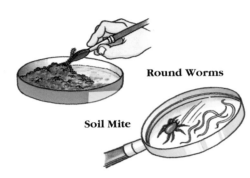

Round Worms

Soil Mite

Measure out a square metre of soil and then scoop up its top layer. In it will be millions of minute animals. Try to find some of them by putting a little of the soil in a dish with some water. Pick up the creatures on a paint brush and use a magnifying glass to examine them.

Underground slugs

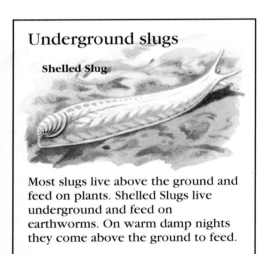

Shelled Slug

Most slugs live above the ground and feed on plants. Shelled Slugs live underground and feed on earthworms. On warm damp nights they come above the ground to feed.

Food webs

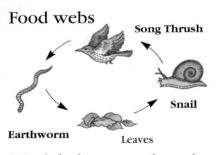

Song Thrush

Snail

Earthworm

Leaves

Animals feed on one another and on plants. This picture shows how the earthworm and snail feed on leaves. In turn, these two animals are eaten by thrushes. Feeding patterns like this are called food webs. Most animals eat a variety of foods, so food webs are usually more complicated than this.

Worms

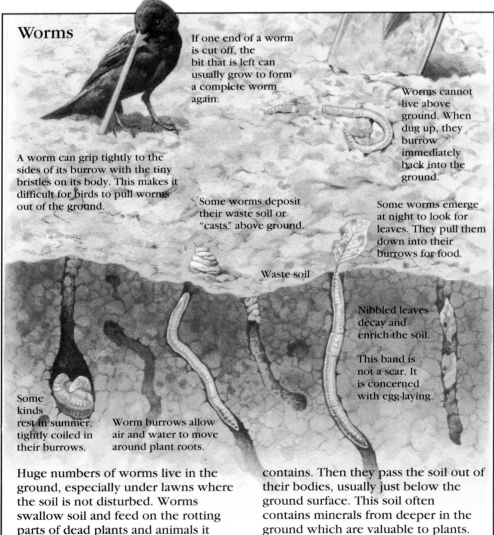

If one end of a worm is cut off, the bit that is left can usually grow to form a complete worm again.

A worm can grip tightly to the sides of its burrow with the tiny bristles on its body. This makes it difficult for birds to pull worms out of the ground.

Worms cannot live above ground. When dug up, they burrow immediately back into the ground.

Some worms deposit their waste soil or "casts" above ground.

Some worms emerge at night to look for leaves. They pull them down into their burrows for food.

Waste soil

Nibbled leaves decay and enrich the soil.

This band is not a scar. It is concerned with egg-laying.

Some kinds rest in summer, tightly coiled in their burrows.

Worm burrows allow air and water to move around plant roots.

Huge numbers of worms live in the ground, especially under lawns where the soil is not disturbed. Worms swallow soil and feed on the rotting parts of dead plants and animals it contains. Then they pass the soil out of their bodies, usually just below the ground surface. This soil often contains minerals from deeper in the ground which are valuable to plants.

Animals that come out of the ground

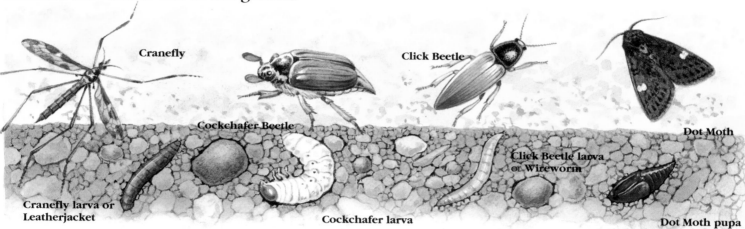

Cranefly

Cockchafer Beetle

Click Beetle

Dot Moth

Cranefly larva or Leatherjacket

Cockchafer larva

Click Beetle larva or Wireworm

Dot Moth pupa

Several insects found in gardens start life in the soil. For example, some beetles and flies lay their eggs in soil. When the young insects, called larvae, hatch they feed on plant roots. It may be several years before the adult insects emerge above ground. Some moth caterpillars form pupae (see page 110) in the soil. If you dig up a pupa, try keeping it in a cool place until the adult moth emerges. Put the pupa on sand in a box with a few twigs and check it every day.

Moles

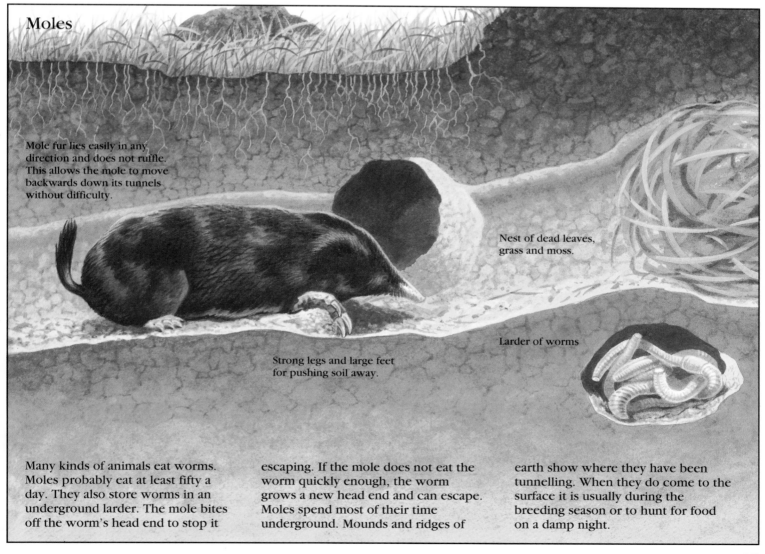

Mole fur lies easily in any direction and does not ruffle. This allows the mole to move backwards down its tunnels without difficulty.

Nest of dead leaves, grass and moss.

Larder of worms

Strong legs and large feet for pushing soil away.

Many kinds of animals eat worms. Moles probably eat at least fifty a day. They also store worms in an underground larder. The mole bites off the worm's head end to stop it escaping. If the mole does not eat the worm quickly enough, the worm grows a new head end and can escape. Moles spend most of their time underground. Mounds and ridges of earth show where they have been tunnelling. When they do come to the surface it is usually during the breeding season or to hunt for food on a damp night.

How to attract wildlife

A neat, tidy garden with no overgrown patches gives little shelter to wildlife. A small corner of long grass and nettles, where dead plants are left to rot instead of being cleared away, attracts many insects. These insects then attract visits from larger animals that feed on them.

You could create your own habitats where animals can hide, build their nests or hibernate. You could also grow some of the plants, shown here and on page 111, which provide food for insects and birds.

Some flowers, such as **Michaelmas Daisies**, attract butterflies to feed on their nectar.

Some climbing plants give food and shelter to animals. In spring birds may build their nests in them, and in winter feed on any berries. The Holly Blue Butterfly survives the winter as a pupa (see page 110) in Ivy leaves.

Wedge a flower pot or an old jug in a hedge or bank to provide a nesting site for birds. Put some dried grass in it.

Magpie

Song Thrush

Ivy

Wren

Holly Blue Butterfly

Cotoneaster

Peacock Butterfly

If you leave a fallen log or branch on the ground, fungi and mosses will grow on it, while beetles and other small animals will live in the decaying wood.

Leave fallen fruit for butterflies and wasps to feed on.

Dead leaves under a hedge or shrub might encourage a Hedgehog to hibernate there.

Some bees and wasps live alone in small holes, such as those in a ventilation brick. You could put one in your garden.

Nesting materials

Wool

Animal hair

Feathers

Moss

Dry grass

Scraps of material.

In spring, attract birds to your garden by hanging up nesting materials from a tree. You could put them in a plastic fruit net.

Solitary Bee

Mournful Wasp

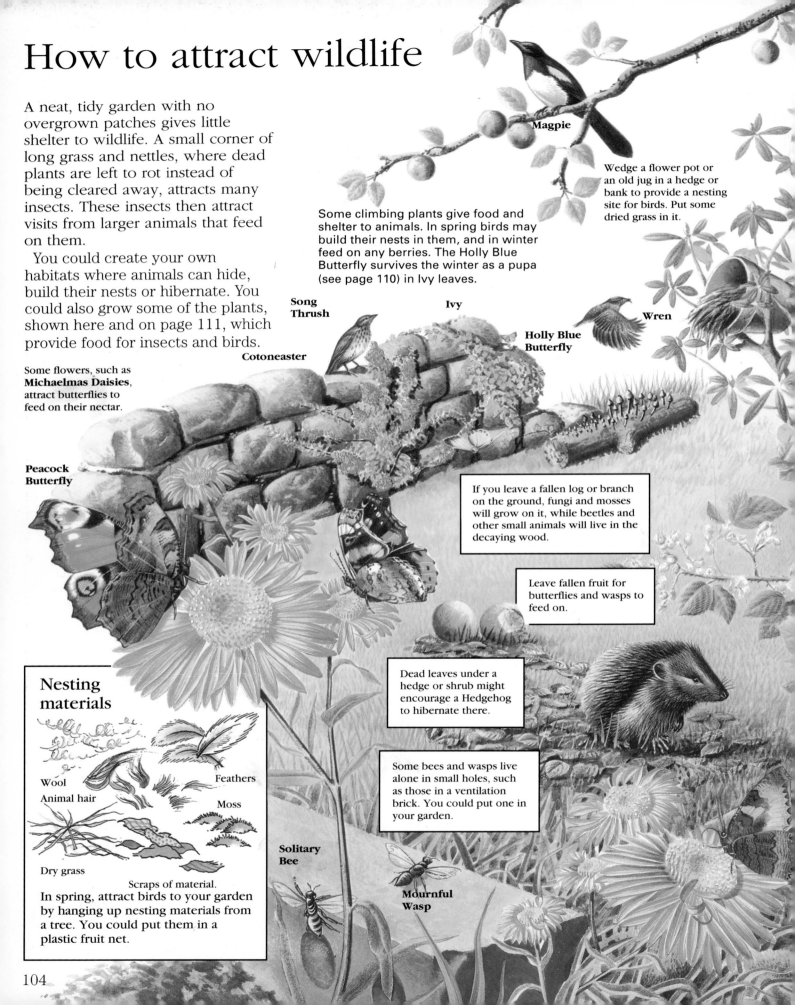

The wildlife on these pages is not drawn to scale.

Feeding birds

A bird table in your garden will attract many different types of birds, especially in winter. To make this simple bird table, use a piece of plywood for the base and thin strips of wood for the edges. To make a roof for the table, use another piece of plywood and a thick strip of wood to support it. Fix the table to a post or hang it from a tree. Remember to wash it regularly.

Hang on a sturdy branch.

Screw-eye

Food

Bacon

Bread

Dried fruit

Cooked potato

Cheese

Banana

Shelled peanuts in a net bag (not salted).

These are some foods that birds like to eat. Collect seeds for them to eat in the winter. Try thistles, groundsel and other wild plants, together with berries like hips and haws, and nuts like acorns.

Water

Dustbin lid

Bricks

Dangers to wildlife

Pest-killers do not only kill the creatures they are meant to kill. They are also likely to poison other animals that feed in the same area. Animals are also harmed when they eat the poisoned creatures.

Slug pellets

Chemical spray

A piece of corrugated iron or a plank of wood on rough grass could shelter a toad, Slow Worms, beetles or a Field Mouse's nest.

Common Toad

Devil's Coach Horse Beetle

Bird table

Nail or screw support to roof and table.

Glue and screw, or nail, edge pieces to table.

Roof keeps the rain off, and encourages smaller birds to feed.

Leave gaps for rain to drain off.

To hang your table from a tree, fix a screw-eye at each corner and make two loops with thick string. When you put food out on the table, put some on the ground as well, for ground-feeding birds. Keep a record of the types of food different birds eat.

Peanuts on a string.

Make a hole in the bottom of the pot and thread string through to hang up.

You can make a bird pudding by mixing kitchen scraps and uncooked porridge oats with melted fat. (Ask an adult to melt the fat.) Carefully pour the mixture into an empty yoghurt pot. Hang the pot upside down.

Birds need water for drinking and bathing all through the year. Use an old tin tray, a dustbin lid or a pie dish. Change the water daily and keep it free of ice in winter.

Cats scare and attack birds. They also attack small mammals such as mice, voles and shrews.

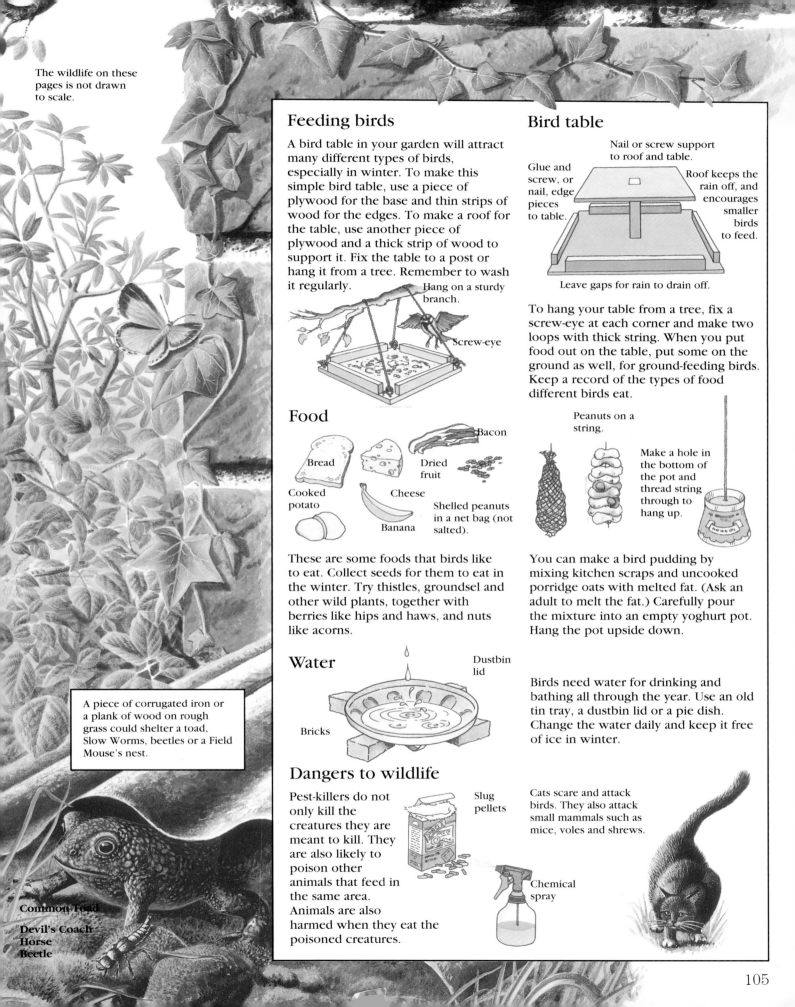

Collared Dove

Greenfinches and **Blue Tits** are common visitors to gardens when food is put out for them. (See page 105.)

Blue Tits

The **Goldfinch** feeds on plant seeds, but attacks Dandelion flowers in spring.

The birds on these pages are not to scale.

Spot the difference

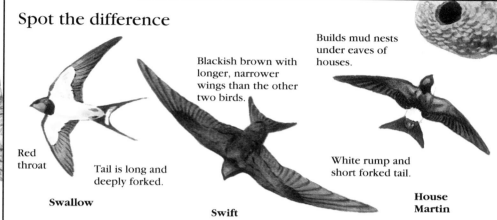

Red throat

Tail is long and deeply forked.

Swallow

Blackish brown with longer, narrower wings than the other two birds.

Swift

Builds mud nests under eaves of houses.

White rump and short forked tail.

House Martin

These birds, which are all summer visitors to Britain, look rather similar. The pictures will help you to identify them. All three catch insects while flying, but they feed at different heights. The Swallows feeds near the ground and is often seen swooping low over water. The House Martin's flight is less swooping and it feeds higher than the Swallow. The Swift feeds much higher in the air than the other two birds.

Catching insects

Spotted Flycatcher

The Spotted Flycatcher, another summer visitor, sits on a tree or post and waits for insects to pass nearby. It flies off to catch its prey, then returns to its perch.

Anting

Mistle Thrush covered with ants.

Some birds rub ants on their feathers or allow ants to crawl over them. They probably do this because a liquid from the ants helps to clean their feathers and rid them of mites.

Roosting

At night, many birds gather together in large numbers for warmth and safety. The tree or building they settle on for the night is called a "roost". Birds may fly many miles each evening to the same roost. In Britain, it is quite common to see thousands of Starlings roosting together often in the middle of towns.

Ponds & trees

Ponds and trees attract all kinds of wildlife. Many insects will live in or on the water, and frogs and toads may breed there. Birds will come to drink and bathe, and hunt for insects, especially if you put a stone for them to perch on.

As more and more farm ponds are being drained, valuable water habitats are lost. Garden ponds can help to replace them. Trees attract all kinds of wildlife too. Choose a tree in your garden, or in a park, and count how many different kinds of creatures you can spot.

Making a pond

Pond should be at least 1 m long, 70 cm wide and 40 cm deep.

Thick layer of newspaper or sand.

It is quite easy to make a small pond in the garden. Start by digging a hole with gently sloping sides. Then make a shallow shelf around the edge for border plants. Smooth the sides and bottom, and remove any sharp stones.

Place sand or a thick layer of newspaper over the sides and bottom of the hole. Line the pond with strong polythene, which you can buy at a garden centre. Weight the edge of the plastic down with stones.

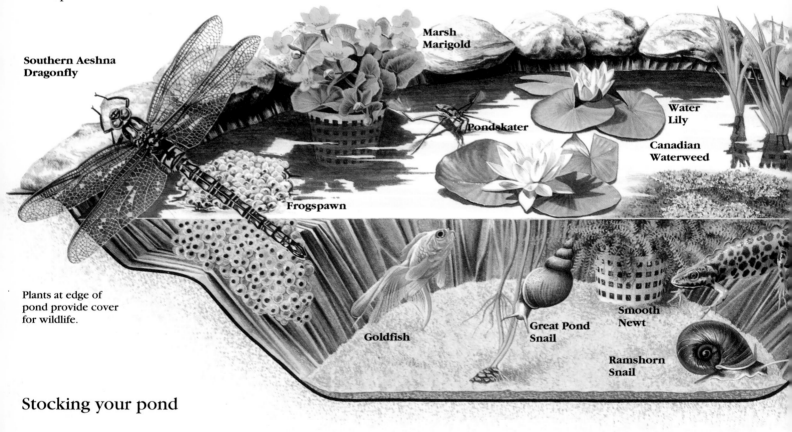

Southern Aeshna Dragonfly

Marsh Marigold

Pondskater

Water Lily

Canadian Waterweed

Frogspawn

Plants at edge of pond provide cover for wildlife.

Goldfish

Great Pond Snail

Smooth Newt

Ramshorn Snail

Stocking your pond

Fill the pond with fresh water and buy some water plants from a garden centre. Plants, such as Canadian Waterweed, are important as they provide oxygen, which fish and other animals need to breathe. Floating plants, such as Water Lilies, provide shade from the sun.

Stock the pond with fish and snails.

Other animals, especially insects, will visit the pond to feed and breed. Some insects, such as dragonflies, start life in ponds but leave the water when fully grown. The adults return to water to lay their eggs. Look out for other winged insects hunting for food around the pond. Frogs, toads and newts spend most of their adult life

on land. You may find them hiding in damp corners in your garden. In spring, they go to ponds to mate and lay their jelly-covered eggs, called spawn. Frogspawn is laid in clusters and toadspawn is laid in strings. When the tadpoles hatch, they stay in the water until their lungs and legs develop. Then they can survive on dry land.

This picture gives you an idea of the kind of wildlife you may find on a tree. You won't find all these things together, as shown here.

Trees provide food and shelter for many different kinds of animals. No matter what size or type a tree is, birds and all sorts of insects and small creatures will use it.

Trees in Britain are either broadleaved, with wide flat leaves, or conifers, with needle-like leaves.

Squirrels live in trees and are active by day. They feed on tree seeds and nuts. You are more likely to see Grey Squirrels in Britain, but on the continent you will only see Red Squirrels.

Many birds nest and roost in trees.

If you find an oak tree, look inside the galls for insect larvae.

Look for caterpillars on leaves and twigs.

Yellow Flag

Common Frog

Water Boatman

Put some stones on shelf for animals to climb onto, and for birds to perch on.

Climbing plants, such as Ivy and Honeysuckle, grow up tree trunks. They provide food shelter for animals.

Bracket fungi grow on tree trunks.

Some moths rest on tree trunks during the day. Beetles and other insects live in cracks and behind loose bark.

If you leave fallen leaves on the ground around trees, insects will hide and feed there. Birds will then come to hunt for the insects.

Fungi may grow among dead leaves in autumn.

The wildlife on these pages is not drawn to scale.

If you have a fruit tree, leave a few of the fruits on the ground to attract butterflies and other insects that feed on the juice of fruit.

121

The garden at night

Many animals (called nocturnal animals) are active only at night. Some come out at dusk, others emerge later and move around until dawn. Go into your garden at these times, with a torch covered in red tissue paper, to see what you can find.

Some nocturnal animals are noisy, so listen carefully and you may hear a grunting Hedgehog or a croaking Toad.

The flowers of some plants, such as Honeysuckle, produce a strong scent at dusk to attract the feeding moths.

The wildlife on these pages is not drawn to scale.

The **Green Lacewing** lives on trees and bushes. The larvae and adults feed on aphids.

The male **Dark Bush-cricket** chirps loudly on summer evenings to attract female crickets.

Glow-worms are beetles. On summer nights, the glow produced by the wingless females attracts the winged males flying above.

The **Tawny Owl** is the most-common owl in gardens. It hunts at night for mice and other small animals, and may even attack birds while they roost.

The **Common Toad** hunts at night for insects and slugs. It always returns to the same place, usually a hole in the ground, to hide during the day.

The **Hedgehog** is a noisy animal and grunts as it hunts for food at night. If you spot one, you can encourage it to return by putting out a saucer of water and some cat or dog food.

The **Wood Mouse** comes out only when it is very dark. It feeds mainly on seeds and berries and will climb bushes to reach fruit.

Ground Beetles hunt for slugs and other small creatures at night.

At night, moths use the moon's light as a guide to fly in a straight line. They do this by keeping the moon's light on the same side of their body. Put a bright light in the garden at night which will attract moths, and then watch how they react. As they pass nearby, the moths are confused by the light and try to use it to steer by. Keeping the light on the same side of their body, they fly in a circle, getting closer to the light until finally they fly into it.

Bats are active at dusk and just before sunrise. They feed on insects.

Pipistrelle Bat (above)

Long-eared Bat (below)

Foxes hunt at night for small animals and birds. They may visit gardens to scavenge for food in dustbins. They have a strong, musty smell.

Some beetles fly at dusk. They are often attracted to lights and may crash into windows.

The **Common Shrew** needs to eat its own weight in food every day. It spends most of its time hunting for food in hedgerows and long grass and only comes out into the open at night.

Elephant Hawk Moth drinks **Honeysuckle** nectar. **Heart and Dart Moth** on **Evening Primrose**. **Silver-Y Moth** on **Night Scented Stock**. **Burnished Brass Moth** on **Valerian**.

C Insects without wings

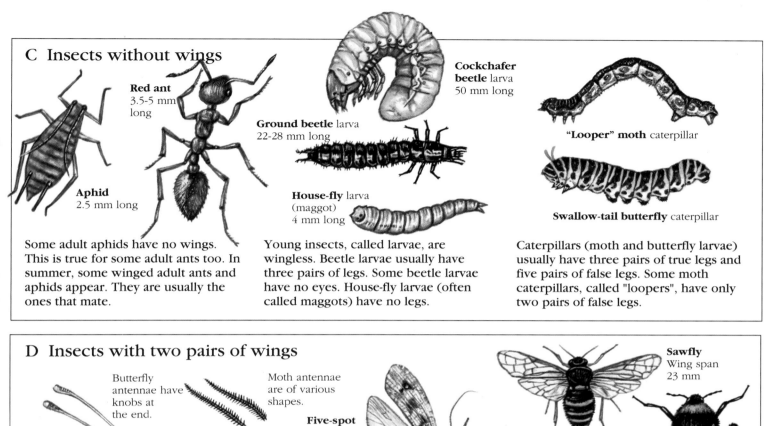

Red ant
3.5-5 mm
long

Aphid
2.5 mm long

Cockchafer beetle larva
50 mm long

Ground beetle larva
22-28 mm long

House-fly larva
(maggot)
4 mm long

"Looper" moth caterpillar

Swallow-tail butterfly caterpillar

Some adult aphids have no wings. This is true for some adult ants too. In summer, some winged adult ants and aphids appear. They are usually the ones that mate.

Young insects, called larvae, are wingless. Beetle larvae usually have three pairs of legs. Some beetle larvae have no eyes. House-fly larvae (often called maggots) have no legs.

Caterpillars (moth and butterfly larvae) usually have three pairs of true legs and five pairs of false legs. Some moth caterpillars, called "loopers", have only two pairs of false legs.

D Insects with two pairs of wings

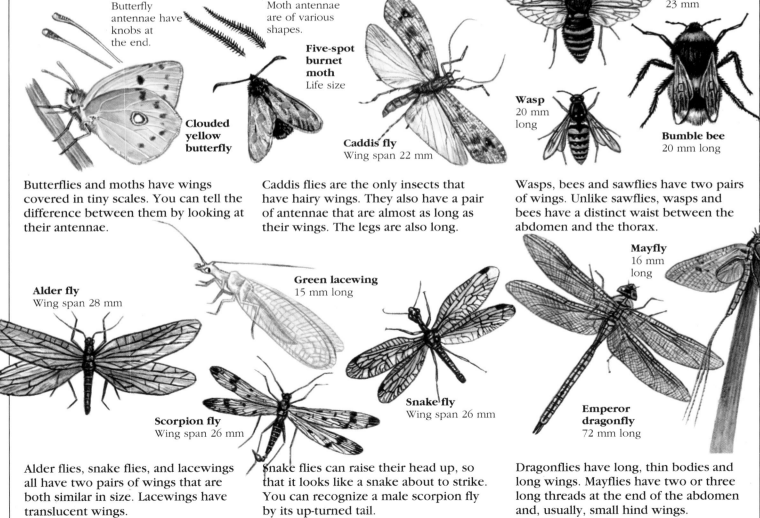

Butterfly antennae have knobs at the end.

Moth antennae are of various shapes.

Five-spot burnet moth
Life size

Clouded yellow butterfly

Caddis fly
Wing span 22 mm

Sawfly
Wing span
23 mm

Wasp
20 mm
long

Bumble bee
20 mm long

Butterflies and moths have wings covered in tiny scales. You can tell the difference between them by looking at their antennae.

Caddis flies are the only insects that have hairy wings. They also have a pair of antennae that are almost as long as their wings. The legs are also long.

Wasps, bees and sawflies have two pairs of wings. Unlike sawflies, wasps and bees have a distinct waist between the abdomen and the thorax.

Alder fly
Wing span 28 mm

Green lacewing
15 mm long

Scorpion fly
Wing span 26 mm

Snake fly
Wing span 26 mm

Mayfly
16 mm
long

Emperor dragonfly
72 mm long

Alder flies, snake flies, and lacewings all have two pairs of wings that are both similar in size. Lacewings have translucent wings.

Snake flies can raise their head up, so that it looks like a snake about to strike. You can recognize a male scorpion fly by its up-turned tail.

Dragonflies have long, thin bodies and long wings. Mayflies have two or three long threads at the end of the abdomen and, usually, small hind wings.

Breeding, growing and changing

Most insects hatch from eggs. After they have hatched, they go through different stages of growth before becoming adults. Some young insects change shape completely before they are adult. Others just get bigger.

Insects such as crickets, earwigs, grasshoppers and bugs, hatch from the eggs looking like small adults. They have no wings when they hatch and are called nymphs. They moult several times, growing bigger each time. The nymph has small wing buds which expand into wings at the last moult.

Other insects change so much that when they hatch they do not look at all like the adults they will become.

The young of these types of insect, such as butterflies, moths, beetles, flies, ants and bees, are called larvae. A caterpillar is the larva of a moth or butterfly. Larvae moult several times as they grow.

When these larvae have grown to a certain size, they shed their skin for the last time and become pupae. Pupae do not feed and usually do not move. Inside the pupa, the body of the young insect slowly changes into an adult.

When the adult is ready to emerge, the pupal skin splits and the adult struggles out. It does not grow after this.

All insects have a soft skin at first, but this hardens and then cannot stretch. As they grow, insects have to change their skin by moulting.

A new skin grows under the old one. The old skin splits and the insect wriggles out, covered in its new, larger skin. Once the insect has become adult, it does not grow any more.

Dragonflies

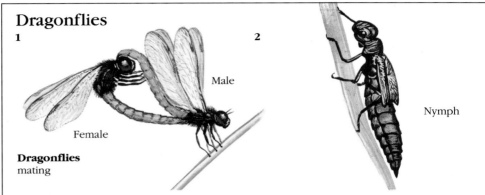

1

Male
Female

Dragonflies
mating

These dragonflies are mating. The male holds on to the neck of the female. The female lays her eggs either straight on the water or on a water plant. Nymphs hatch from the eggs.

2

Nymph

Dragonfly nymphs live in the water for two years or more. When they moult, they change colour to blend in with their surroundings. They crawl onto a stem before they moult into an adult.

3

Adult
dragonfly

Old skin

Here, the adult dragonfly is emerging from the nymph. The skin of the nymph has split and first the head and then the thorax of the adult appear. The old skin still clings to the stem.

4

Adult
dragonfly

Old skin

After a short rest, the adult dragonfly pulls its abdomen out of the old skin. Then it rests on the stem by hanging from its legs, while its body gains shape and the wings expand.

Grasshoppers

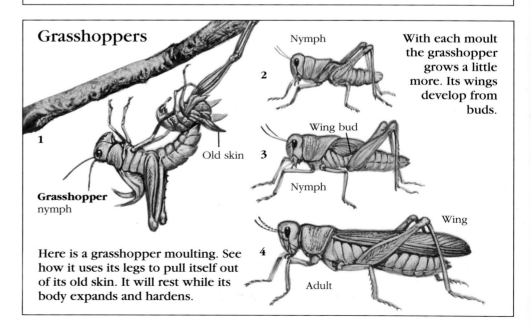

Nymph

2

With each moult the grasshopper grows a little more. Its wings develop from buds.

1

Old skin

Grasshopper
nymph

Wing bud

3

Nymph

Here is a grasshopper moulting. See how it uses its legs to pull itself out of its old skin. It will rest while its body expands and hardens.

4

Wing

Adult

Mating

The adults of all types of insects mate with other insects of the same species. Then the females lay their eggs. Some are laid on stems, some are laid in or on the ground, and some in water.

Usually the eggs are laid on or near food that the larvae can feed on. The bluebottle eggs in the picture below have been laid on a dead animal. The larvae will feed on the animal when they hatch.

Lacewings lay their eggs on the end of a stalk that is made with special gum from the abdomen. It is thought that this method protects the eggs from ants that like to eat them.

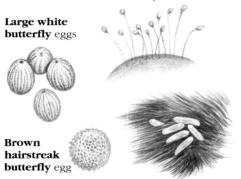

Lacewing eggs on stalks made of gum by female.

Large white butterfly eggs

Brown hairstreak butterfly egg

Bluebottle eggs

Female insects lay their eggs either singly, like the brown hairstreak butterfly, or in clusters, like the bluebottle and lacewing. A few insects leave the eggs once they are laid.

Gnats

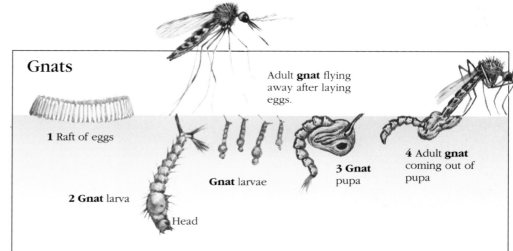

1 Raft of eggs

2 Gnat larva

Head

Gnat larvae

Adult **gnat** flying away after laying eggs.

3 Gnat pupa

4 Adult gnat coming out of pupa

Gnats lay their eggs in groups, which float like a raft on the water's surface (1). The larvae (2) hatch out, and hang from the surface, breathing air through a siphon. Each larva turns into a pupa (3), which also lives near the surface. When the adult has formed inside the pupa, the skin splits and it crawls out (4).

Butterflies

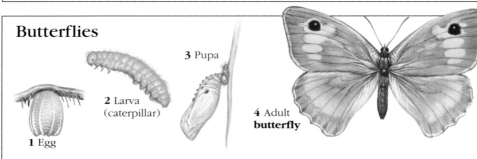

1 Egg

2 Larva (caterpillar)

3 Pupa

4 Adult **butterfly**

The meadow brown butterfly lays a single egg on grass (1). The caterpillar (2) hatches and spends the winter in this form. Early the next summer, it turns into a pupa (3).

Inside the pupa, or chrysalis, the body of the caterpillar breaks down and then becomes the body of the butterfly. This takes about four weeks. Then the pupa splits, and the adult emerges. It rests while its crumpled wings spread out and dry. Then it is ready to fly (4).

Stag beetles

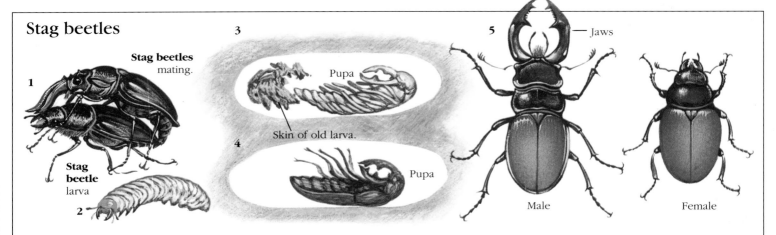

1 **Stag beetles** mating.

2 **Stag beetle** larva

3 Pupa

Skin of old larva.

4 Pupa

5 Jaws

Male

Female

After mating (1), the female stag beetle lays her eggs in the holes of rotten trees. The young larva (2) lives for three years, burrowing through the tree's soft wood. Then, the larva stops feeding, makes a pupal cell in the wood and becomes a pupa (3). It lies on its back to protect the newly-formed limbs until they harden (4). Then it emerges as an adult beetle (5). The males have large jaws that they use for fighting and to attract the females.

Insects in the garden

A good place to start a study of insects is your own garden. If you do not have a garden then look in a park or open green space. Make a chart of the insects you find there each month. Look under stones, on the bark of trees, on plants and grass, and among dead leaves. It is even worth looking in a garden shed.

Some insects spend the winter without moving or feeding. This is called hibernation. Make a note of where you find hibernating insects, but never disturb them.

1 On tree trunks

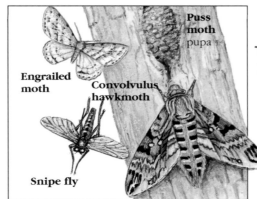

Moths, especially ones that are the colour of bark, rest on trees. In winter, look for pupae in bark crevices.

2 Under bark

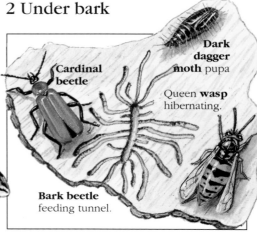

Queen wasps and beetles sometimes hibernate under loose bark. Look for bark beetle tunnels in the bark.

6 In wood piles

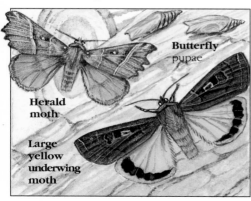

These insects hibernate in sheltered spots like wood piles in winter. Take great care not to disturb them.

7 On walls

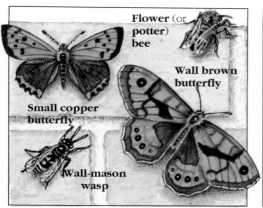

These insects can often be found on walls where they like to settle, particularly if the walls face the sun.

8 In the rubbish heap

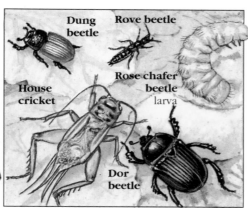

These insects feed on waste matter, such as animal droppings. You are most likely to find them in a rubbish heap.

9 Under stones

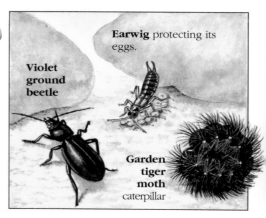

Lift up large stones and you will probably discover these insects. They like to live in dark, damp places.

3 On leaves and stems

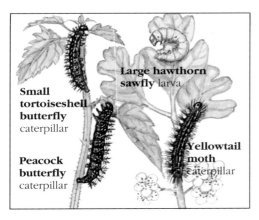

Small tortoiseshell butterfly caterpillar

Large hawthorn sawfly larva

Peacock butterfly caterpillar

Yellowtail moth caterpillar

Most caterpillars feed on leaves. Spot them in spring and summer, particularly on hedges and bushes.

4 Houses and sheds

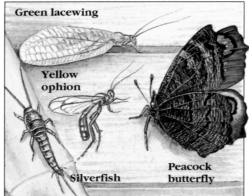

Green lacewing

Yellow ophion

Silverfish

Peacock butterfly

If you search a shed in winter, you may find a peacock butterfly or a green lacewing hibernating.

5 On grasses

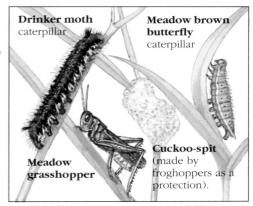

Drinker moth caterpillar

Meadow brown butterfly caterpillar

Meadow grasshopper

Cuckoo-spit (made by froghoppers as a protection).

Search carefully for insects on grasses. Many of them are green and blend in with surroundings, so are difficult to see.

The insect watcher's code

When looking for insects remember the insect watcher's code.

Always replace logs and stones exactly as you found them. They are often the homes of insects.

Search carefully and try not to damage flowers and twigs, and never peel the bark off trees.

You have a better chance of finding insects if you move slowly and quietly.

You can discover a lot just by waiting and watching.

10 In the soil

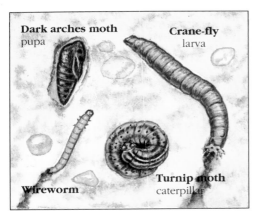

Dark arches moth pupa

Crane-fly larva

Wireworm

Turnip moth caterpillar

Some insects, such as these, live in the soil. You will have to dig to find them. The larvae feed on roots.

11 On flowers

Silver-washed fritillary

Hornet

In summer, you will see insects such as these feeding on the nectar and pollen of flowers.

12 On the ground

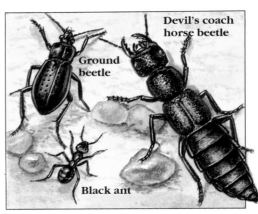

Devil's coach horse beetle

Ground beetle

Black ant

Watch ants and beetles scuttling over the ground in summer. See if you can follow them and spot where they go.

Insects in a tree

Thousands of different types of insect live in and on trees. You can make a study of the insects you find on one type of tree. The tree on this page is a common oak.

Try to choose a tree that stands on its own away from other trees. Make a note of how many kinds of insect you spot, where you find them on the tree and what the season is. See if you can identify them and discover some facts about them.

Is there a connection between the kinds of insect you find and the leaves, flowers or fruits on the tree? Compare the kinds of insect you find on your tree with those on other types of tree. Make a note of the differences and see if you can discover why each type of tree is better suited to certain insects.

Moth caterpillars

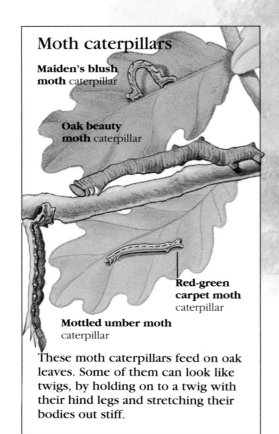

Maiden's blush moth caterpillar

Oak beauty moth caterpillar

Red-green carpet moth caterpillar

Mottled umber moth caterpillar

These moth caterpillars feed on oak leaves. Some of them can look like twigs, by holding on to a twig with their hind legs and stretching their bodies out stiff.

Greenfly

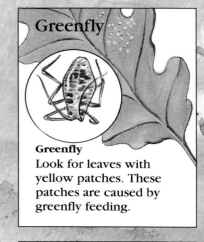

Greenfly
Look for leaves with yellow patches. These patches are caused by greenfly feeding.

Moths

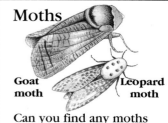

Goat moth

Leopard moth

Can you find any moths resting on the tree trunk? Their colouring can make them difficult to see.

Weevils

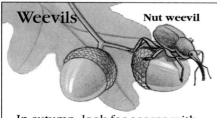

Nut weevil

In autumn, look for acorns with holes in them. These are where weevils have laid eggs. The female bores a tunnel into the acorn with her long nose and then places the egg at the end of it. The weevil larva feeds on the acorn.

Bark beetles

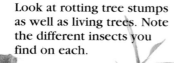

Pupal chamber

Oak bark beetle

Egg tunnel

Larvae feeding tunnels.

The female bark beetle bores a tunnel for her eggs. When the larvae hatch they bore tunnels at right angles to the main tunnel. They make a pupal chamber at the end, from which they emerge as adults.

Dig the soil a few metres from the tree and see what insects you can find there.

Look at rotting tree stumps as well as living trees. Note the different insects you find on each.

Green oak-roller

Green oak-roller moth

If disturbed, the caterpillar can lower itself on a silken thread.

The caterpillar hides and feeds inside an oak leaf, which it rolls over and binds with silk.

Carrion beetles

This four-spot carrion beetle feeds on green oak-roller moth caterpillars.

Beetles

Cockchafer beetle

Longhorn beetle

Cockchafer beetles eat the leaves of trees and other plants. Longhorn beetles lay their eggs in crevices in the bark.

Feeding

Common goldeneye lacewing

10-spot ladybird

Lacewings and ladybirds feed on aphids such as greenfly that live on oak trees.

Bugs

Capsid bug

There are many types of capsid bug. Some like to live on oak trees. They feed on the sap of the leaves, or on young acorns.

Watch for birds eating insects on trees.

Oak apple galls

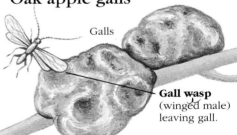

Galls

Gall wasp (winged male) leaving gall.

In May, you can see oak apple galls like these. They are made by gall wasp larvae. The adult wasps emerge in mid-summer.

Look in the leaf litter on the ground beneath the tree for larvae and pupae.

Moth larva

Common swift moth caterpillars feed on the young roots of trees, and other plants. They pupate in the soil.

Beetle larva

Cockchafer larvae live in the soil for at least three years. They feed on the roots of trees and are very destructive to young trees.

Gall wasps

Gall

Gall wasp (wingless female)

Gall wasps lay their eggs in oak roots. Galls form with larvae inside. Wingless females emerge and crawl up the tree to lay their eggs in the buds, which swell into oak apples.

Honey bees

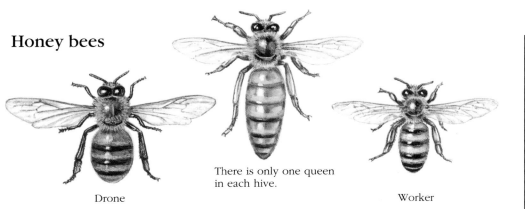

Drone

There is only one queen in each hive.

Worker

These are three different kinds of honey bee that you will find in a bee hive. The only honey bees you will see flying around are the workers. The others stay only in the hive.

The workers do all the jobs. Young workers clean out cells, then as they get older, they feed the larvae, build new cells and make honey. Later they collect nectar and pollen.

The honeycomb

This is what the inside of a honey bee's comb looks like. It is made of six-sided wax cells. Those near the outside are for breeding drones and for storing honey. Those in the middle are brood cells for worker bees. Pollen is packed in cells next to the brood cells. Queen bee larvae have special cells.

Royal jelly

Queen bee larva

Capped **queen cell** cut away to show larva inside.

Uncapped **brood cell** containing egg or larva of worker bee.

Brood cell, capped, with larva inside.

Uncapped **honey cell**.

Cell containing **honey** and **pollen**, which is food for the larvae.

Pollen cell

Cell filled with **honey** and capped with **wax**.

How a bee grows

Comb   Cell

Queen lays egg.

Egg hatches.

Worker feeds larva with a mix of honey and pollen.

Worker seals cell with wax.

Larva changes into pupa.

Pupa grows.

Young worker bee emerges.

The queen lays one egg in each cell. After three days the eggs hatch. The worker bees feed the larvae on a mixture of honey and pollen. Queen bee larvae are fed on a rich mixture of honey and pollen and some other substances, called royal jelly.

After six days the larvae are large and fat and fill their cells. Worker bees seal the cells with wax made in the bodies of the bees. Inside the cells the larvae pupate. Two weeks later the young bees eat through the seal of wax and emerge fully grown. Before the young worker bees fly from the hive, they sometimes have the special job of keeping the air fresh in the hive by fanning their wings.

Collecting and keeping insects

When you find an insect, out in the garden or in some other place, put it in a small tin. Also place in the tin a piece of the plant on which you found the insect. The plant will give the insect some food and help you to identify it.

Number each tin. Write the numbers in your notebook and, against each one, write a description of the insect and where you found it. Was it in a dry or damp place, a sunny or a shady place?

If you want to keep your insects, when you get home you must put them in a place that is as similar as possible to their natural surroundings. You will need containers that are big enough to hold sufficient food and give the insects some room to move around. It is best to use glass or clear plastic containers, then you can see what is happening inside.

It is usually a good idea to put some sand or soil at the bottom, with a stone and some plants. Keep the containers in a cool place away from the sunlight, but not in a draught.

Make sure you have a good supply of fresh food and change it each day. Most caterpillars have their own particular food plant and will not eat anything else. There is no point in collecting them unless you can give them the right food supply.

Look at the insects in your "zoo" every day and record any changes that you see. You could keep a note of how much caterpillars eat and their length, or describe what happens to them when they pupate. See if you can spot different types of behaviour in different types of caterpillars. Watch how they move and eat.

Collecting crawling insects

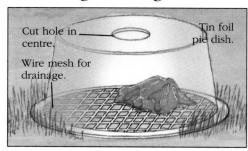

Cut hole in centre.

Tin foil pie dish.

Wire mesh for drainage.

Try making a trap like this. Put bait, such as a piece of meat, in the trap to attract insects. A good place to put the trap is at the bottom of a hedge.

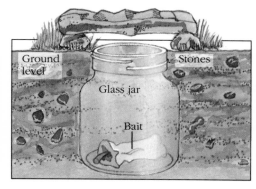

Ground level

Stones

Glass jar

Bait

You could also make a pitfall trap. Try different baits, such as jam, raw meat, fruit or beer. Keep a record of the insects that are attracted by each bait.

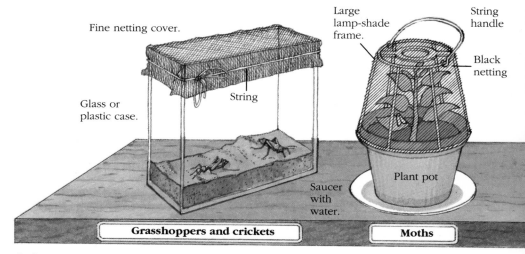

Fine netting cover.

Glass or plastic case.

String

Large lamp-shade frame.

String handle

Black netting

Plant pot

Saucer with water.

Grasshoppers and crickets

Moths

In late summer, you may find crickets and grasshoppers. Keep them in a large glass case or jar with sand in the bottom. Put in fresh grass every other day.

Make a moth cage. Keep it out of the sun and in hot weather spray it with water. If you want the moths to breed, put in the right plant for the larvae to feed on.

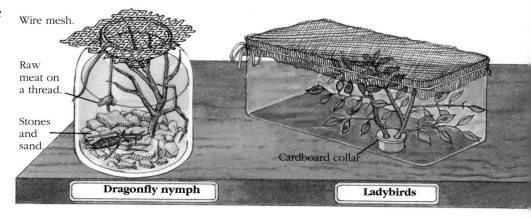

Wire mesh.

Raw meat on a thread.

Stones and sand.

Cardboard collar

Dragonfly nymph

Ladybirds

Keep a dragonfly nymph on its own in a large jam jar and feed it on raw meat. Put in an upright stick for the nymph to cling to when it sheds its skin.

Keep ladybirds in a large case to give them room to fly. They feed on greenfly, often found on rose shoots. Cut off the whole shoot and keep it in water.

Sugaring

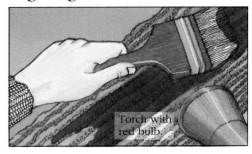
Torch with red bulb.

You can attract moths by "sugaring". Paint tree trunks or posts at dusk with a mixture of black treacle and rum or beer. Warm, still evenings are best.

Lights

Light-traps are used to catch insects. Other lights, such as from a lamp, also attract them. How many can you find that are attracted to light in this way.

Remember

It is easy to collect insects, but remember that they are very fragile. Handle them as little as possible and do not collect more than you need to study.

If you keep the insects for a few days to study, make sure you supply them with a piece of the plant on which you found them.

Never collect a rare or protected species.

Once you have finished looking at them, take the insects back to the place where you found them. Let flying insects go at dusk so that birds or cats do not attack and kill them.

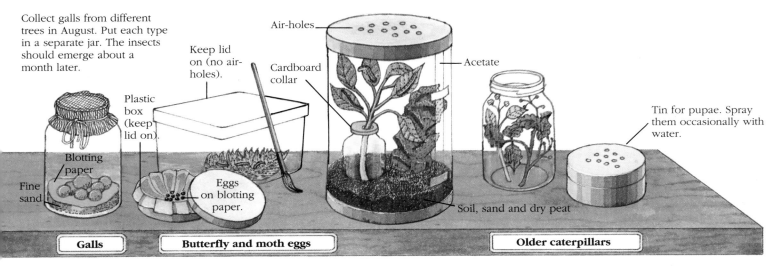

Collect galls from different trees in August. Put each type in a separate jar. The insects should emerge about a month later.

Keep lid on (no air-holes).

Plastic box (keep lid on).

Blotting paper

Fine sand

Eggs on blotting paper.

Air-holes

Cardboard collar

Acetate

Soil, sand and dry peat

Tin for pupae. Spray them occasionally with water.

| Galls | Butterfly and moth eggs | Older caterpillars |

Collect butterfly or moth eggs in small boxes. When the caterpillars hatch, put them in another box and give them a new leaf of their food plant each day.

To make a container for older caterpillars, roll up some acetate and fix it with sticky tape. Put one half of a tin on one end and its lid on the other end.

If you find a caterpillar whose food you do not know, collect several plants. Put them with the caterpillar in a jar. Look after a few hours to see which it eats.

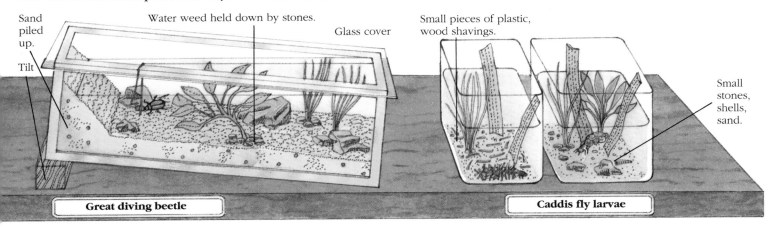

Sand piled up.

Tilt

Water weed held down by stones.

Glass cover

Small pieces of plastic, wood shavings.

Small stones, shells, sand.

| Great diving beetle | Caddis fly larvae |

Great diving beetles and water boatmen are very fierce, so keep each one on its own. Feed them on maggots or raw meat attached to a thread, and change daily.

See how caddis fly larvae make their protective cases. Collect several caddis flies and carefully remove the larvae from their cases by prodding them with

the blunt end of a pin. Put them in separate aquariums with different materials in each, and watch what happens. Feed them on water weed.

Common insects to spot

Butterflies

Red admiral May to June and July to September.

Speckled wood April to June and August to September.

Orange-tip May to June.

Small white May to June and July to August.

Green-veined white May to June and August to September.

Underside of wing.

Common blue May to June and August to September.

Large white May to August.

Wall May to June and August to September.

Meadow brown Mid-June to September.

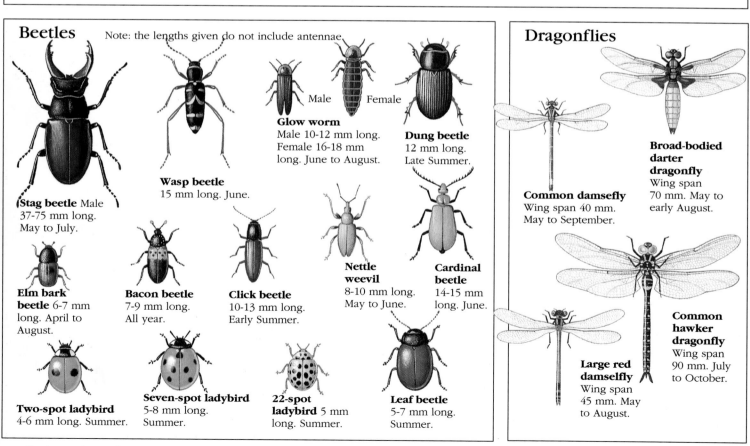

Beetles

Note: the lengths given do not include antennae.

Glow worm
Male 10-12 mm long.
Female 16-18 mm long. June to August.

Male   Female

Dung beetle
12 mm long.
Late Summer.

Wasp beetle
15 mm long. June.

Stag beetle Male 37-75 mm long. May to July.

Elm bark beetle 6-7 mm long. April to August.

Bacon beetle 7-9 mm long. All year.

Click beetle 10-13 mm long. Early Summer.

Nettle weevil 8-10 mm long. May to June.

Cardinal beetle 14-15 mm long. June.

Two-spot ladybird 4-6 mm long. Summer.

Seven-spot ladybird 5-8 mm long. Summer.

22-spot ladybird 5 mm long. Summer.

Leaf beetle 5-7 mm long. Summer.

Dragonflies

Common damselfly
Wing span 40 mm. May to September.

Broad-bodied darter dragonfly
Wing span 70 mm. May to early August.

Large red damselfly
Wing span 45 mm. May to August.

Common hawker dragonfly
Wing span 90 mm. July to October.

Each caption tells you the time of year you are most likely to see the insect. The butterflies and moths are drawn life size. The beetles and dragonflies are not.

Moths

Buff-tip July to August.

Eyed hawkmoth May to July.

Scalloped oak July to August.

Yellowtail July to August.

Small magpie May to mid-July.

Angle shades May to October.

Magpie July to mid-August.

Vapourer Late August to October.

Blood-vein May to September.

Silver-Y Migratory (June to October).

Burnished brass June to September.

Puss moth (male) May to June.

Poplar hawkmoth May to August.

Pale tussock May to June.

Dot June to August.

Brimstone May to June and August to September.

Female

Male

Lackey July to August.

Herald Early spring to autumn.

Ghost swift June to July.

Drinker June to mid-August.

Six-spot burnet Late June to mid-August.

Remember, if you cannot see the insect you want to identify on these pages, turn to the page earlier in the book which deals with the kind of place where you found the insect.

More common insects to spot

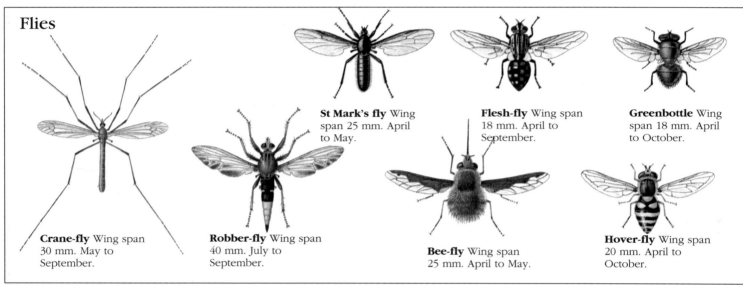

Flies

St Mark's fly Wing span 25 mm. April to May.

Flesh-fly Wing span 18 mm. April to September.

Greenbottle Wing span 18 mm. April to October.

Crane-fly Wing span 30 mm. May to September.

Robber-fly Wing span 40 mm. July to September.

Bee-fly Wing span 25 mm. April to May.

Hover-fly Wing span 20 mm. April to October.

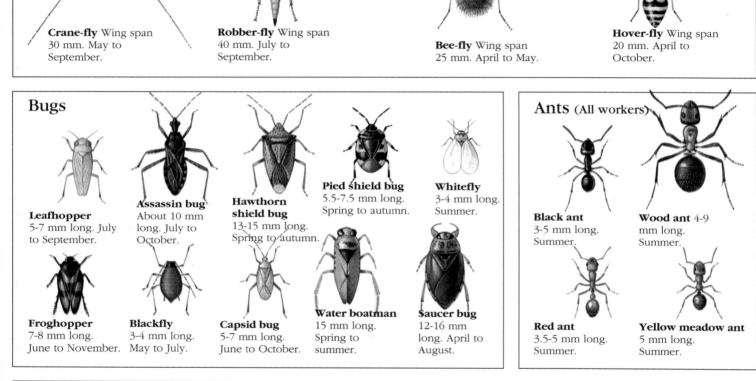

Bugs

Leafhopper 5-7 mm long. July to September.

Assassin bug About 10 mm long. July to October.

Hawthorn shield bug 13-15 mm long. Spring to autumn.

Pied shield bug 5.5-7.5 mm long. Spring to autumn.

Whitefly 3-4 mm long. Summer.

Froghopper 7-8 mm long. June to November.

Blackfly 3-4 mm long. May to July.

Capsid bug 5-7 mm long. June to October.

Water boatman 15 mm long. Spring to summer.

Saucer bug 12-16 mm long. April to August.

Ants (All workers)

Black ant 3-5 mm long. Summer.

Wood ant 4-9 mm long. Summer.

Red ant 3.5-5 mm long. Summer.

Yellow meadow ant 5 mm long. Summer.

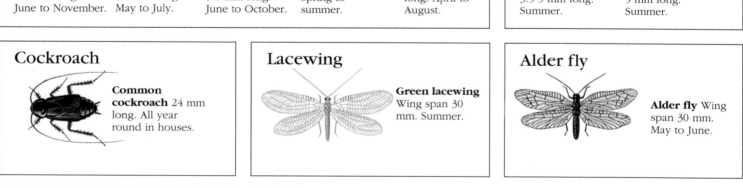

Cockroach

Common cockroach 24 mm long. All year round in houses.

Lacewing

Green lacewing Wing span 30 mm. Summer.

Alder fly

Alder fly Wing span 30 mm. May to June.

Earwig

Common earwig About 16 mm long. All year, especially summer.

Scorpion fly

Common scorpion fly Wing span 30 mm. May to July.

Snake fly

Snake fly Wing span 28 mm. May to July.

158 Each caption tells you the time of year you are most likely to see the insect. The lengths given do not include antennae.

Mayfly

Green drake mayfly Wing span 25 mm. April to September.

Flea

Cat flea 2-3 mm long. All year round.

Grasshoppers and crickets

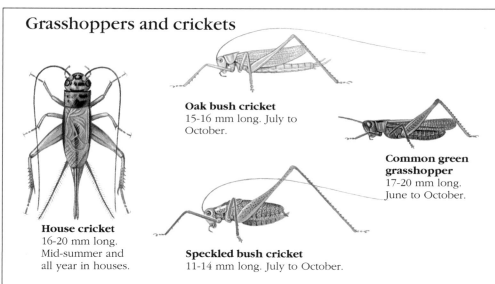

Oak bush cricket 15-16 mm long. July to October.

Common green grasshopper 17-20 mm long. June to October.

House cricket 16-20 mm long. Mid-summer and all year in houses.

Speckled bush cricket 11-14 mm long. July to October.

Thrip

Onion thrip 2 mm long. Summer.

Bristle tail

Silverfish 10 mm long. All year round.

Springtail

Water springtail 2 mm long.

Louse

Book louse 2.5 mm long.

Wasps

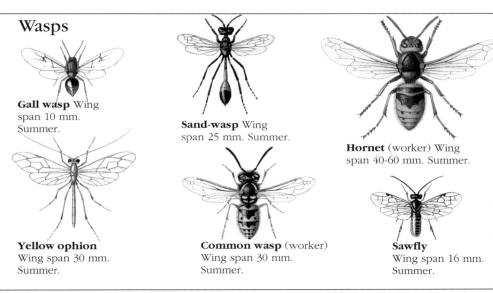

Gall wasp Wing span 10 mm. Summer.

Sand-wasp Wing span 25 mm. Summer.

Hornet (worker) Wing span 40-60 mm. Summer.

Yellow ophion Wing span 30 mm. Summer.

Common wasp (worker) Wing span 30 mm. Summer.

Sawfly Wing span 16 mm. Summer.

Caddis fly

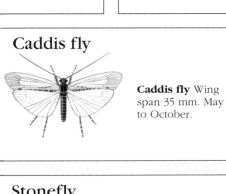

Caddis fly Wing span 35 mm. May to October.

Stonefly

Stonefly Wing span 20 mm. Summer.

Bees (All workers)

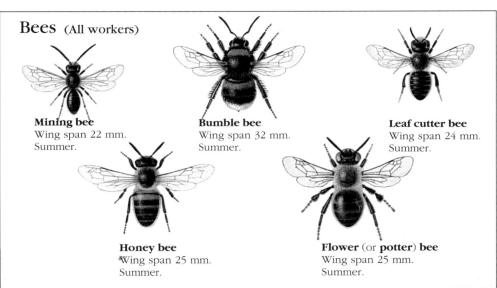

Mining bee Wing span 22 mm. Summer.

Bumble bee Wing span 32 mm. Summer.

Leaf cutter bee Wing span 24 mm. Summer.

Honey bee Wing span 25 mm. Summer.

Flower (or **potter**) **bee** Wing span 25 mm. Summer.

Remember, if you cannot see the insect you want to identify on these pages, turn to the page earlier in the book which deals with the kind of place where you found the insect.

Spiders and their webs

This page shows you some of the interesting things you may see if you go spider-watching. Look for spiders' webs in the early morning when they are covered with frost or dew.

Spiders in bushes can be caught like insects, but in a wood or field, drag a strong bag through the plants and tip the contents out onto a white sheet.

If you want to study spiders closely, have a jam-jar ready to keep them in. Put them back where you found them afterwards.

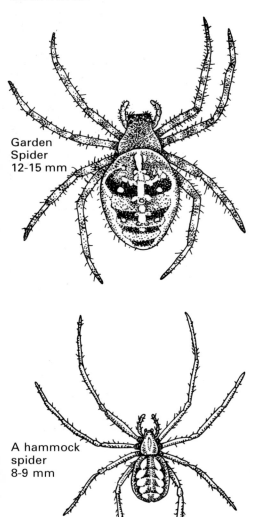

Garden
Spider
12-15 mm

A hammock
spider
8-9 mm

The sizes given are body lengths.

Orb web

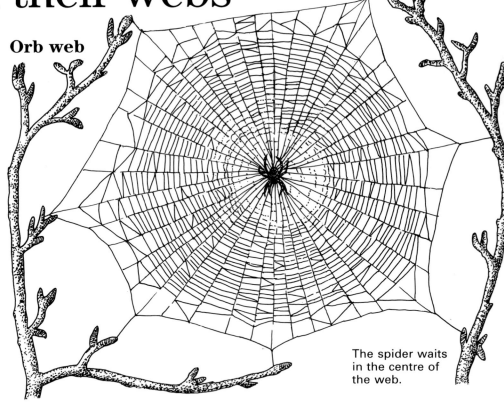

The spider waits in the centre of the web.

This is the orb web of a Garden Spider. You will find it hard to see unless it is covered with dew or frost. Flying insects which bump into the web get caught in the sticky threads.

The spider waiting in the middle feels the vibrations of any trapped insects. It will rush out and paralyse the prey with its poison fangs and then take the insect back to the centre of the web to eat.

Hammock web

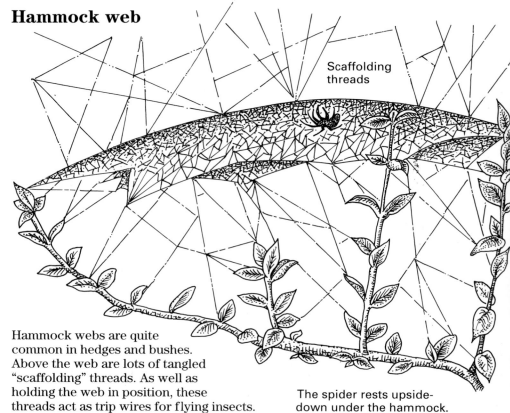

Scaffolding threads

Hammock webs are quite common in hedges and bushes. Above the web are lots of tangled "scaffolding" threads. As well as holding the web in position, these threads act as trip wires for flying insects.

The spider rests upside-down under the hammock.

Sheet web

This is a sheet web made by a house spider. House spiders live behind pictures and in the corners of rooms and sheds. They hide in a silken tube at the corner of the sheet web.

Insects caught in the web.

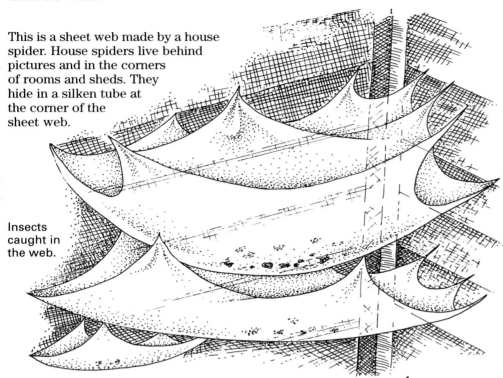

Underwater web

Look in ponds for the Water Spider. To study it properly you will have to keep it in an aquarium for a while.

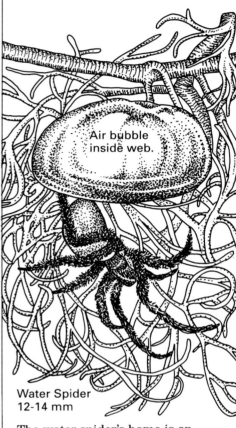

Air bubble inside web.

Water Spider 12-14 mm

The water spider's home is an underwater web attached to water weed. It is rounded and filled with air. The spider fills it by bringing down bubbles of air with its hind legs. It lives inside the bubble, swimming out to catch any passing water insects.

Spiders and their young

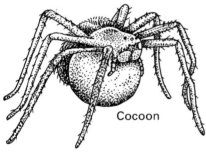

Cocoon

A hunting spider 11-13 mm

Spiders lay eggs which they cover with a cocoon of threads. This hunting spider carries her cocoon with her.

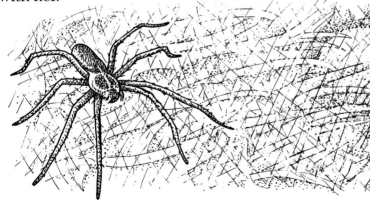

Some spiders spin a protective tent over the cocoon. The spiders hatch inside this "nursery tent" while the mother stands guard.

When the young spiders are ready to live on their own, the mother spider tears open the web to set them free.

Baby spiders

Some spiders that do not have nursery webs carry their young on their backs until the baby spiders can fend for themselves.

161

The fresh water of ponds and streams is a home or hunting ground for many living creatures and plants.

There you will spot the common birds, fish, insects, mammals, plants and amphibians of Europe, all described in this part of the book.

As you turn these pages, you will discover how water animals and plants live and how to collect wild specimens and keep them at home for study.

To identify your fresh-water wildlife, turn to the pages which deal with the kind of animal or plant you have seen. If you can't find a picture of it there, turn to the section called *More freshwater life you can spot* and you may find a picture of it there.

The Usborne Nature Trail Book of

PONDS & STREAMS

Contents

How to start

The best time to study streams and ponds is in the spring and summer, when the plants are flowering and the animals are most active. Winter can be a good time to spot birds though.

Always move slowly and quietly and be careful your shadow does not disturb fish. You will find more wildlife near the bank, where there is more plant cover.

Freshwater life can be found in lakes, rivers, ditches and canals, as well. You may even find plants and insects in rainwater tubs.

Be responsible!

Plants and animals live in harmony with each other and their surroundings. If you remove many plants and animals then you will upset the balance and threaten the survival of some of those that are left behind (see page 167). If you destroy their surroundings (their habitat), you will threaten their survival as well. Never leave litter behind when you leave.

What to take

Clean jam jars

Empty margarine pot for putting animals in and watching them.

Magnifying glass

Fishing net with small mesh.

Binoculars

Safety first

Never go into the water if you cannot swim and only go into shallow water. Do not wade rivers or deep streams. There may be strong currents. Always take a friend or adult with you. If you do fall in and get wet, go straight home to change you clothes and get dry - unless of course it is a very hot sunny day.

A pond survey

With some friends, make a map of your pond, showing where you found certain plants and animals. Note down the types of things going on around the pond and what it is used for, such as boating and fishing, or if cattle drink there. How do all these activities affect the pond? Check for signs of pollution, such as litter and oil.

Note down the animals you see. Record every kind of plant you can see. Look for insects on the plants.

What to look for

Even a small pond or stream can have many plants and animals, if it is not too shaded or polluted. Here are some of the plants you should look for and their hiding places.

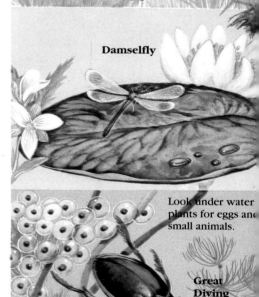

Damselfly

Look under water plants for eggs and small animals.

Great Diving Beetle

In a stream, look under stones for worms, insects and leeches. In a pond, the gaps beneath stones tend to get silted up, so you will not find much wildlife beneath them.

Mayfly nymph

Do's and don'ts

Do test water depth with a long pole before wading in.

Do replace stones and logs exactly as you found them.

Don't handle anything you catch. Put it straight into a dish or jar.

Don't use logs or stones as stepping-stones without testing them first.

Do put animals and plants back into the pond as soon as possible.

Don't stamp your feet or move quickly. This will frighten animals.

Don't take too many animals or whole plants. Part of a plant will be enough to identify it.

Don't smash ice on ponds in winter. This will disturb animals living there.

Do keep jars with specimens in the shade, to keep the water cool.

Even a small pond or stream can have many plants and animals, if it is not too shaded or polluted. Here are some of the plants you should look for and their hiding places.

Remember, wading a pond is very difficult because of the depth of soft mud and rotting leaves at the bottom.

Sweep the net in two or three different spots near the bank and further away from the bank.

Test the water depth with a pole hanging from string or tape held across the pond.

After sweeping the net in the water, put its contents in a pot of clean water and wait for the mud to settle.

Sieving the water with an old tea strainer separates the water animals and plants from the mud. When you have identified the wildlife, put it back.

Measure the distance across the pond and around the pond. Draw the shape on a large sheet of paper. Add the names of plants and animals where you found them.

Look along banks for flowers, reeds and grasses.

Look among reeds for birds' nests. Do not disturb them.

Look on the surface for insects, birds and plants.

Moorhen chick

The **Pond Skater** skims and jumps over the surface.

Look for holes in the banks where animals live.

Look in the water for fish, plants and insects.

Stickleback

Great Crested Newt

Water Shrew

Great Pond Snail

Look on the bottom for animals with shells.

The **Water Spider** lives under the water in an air bubble.

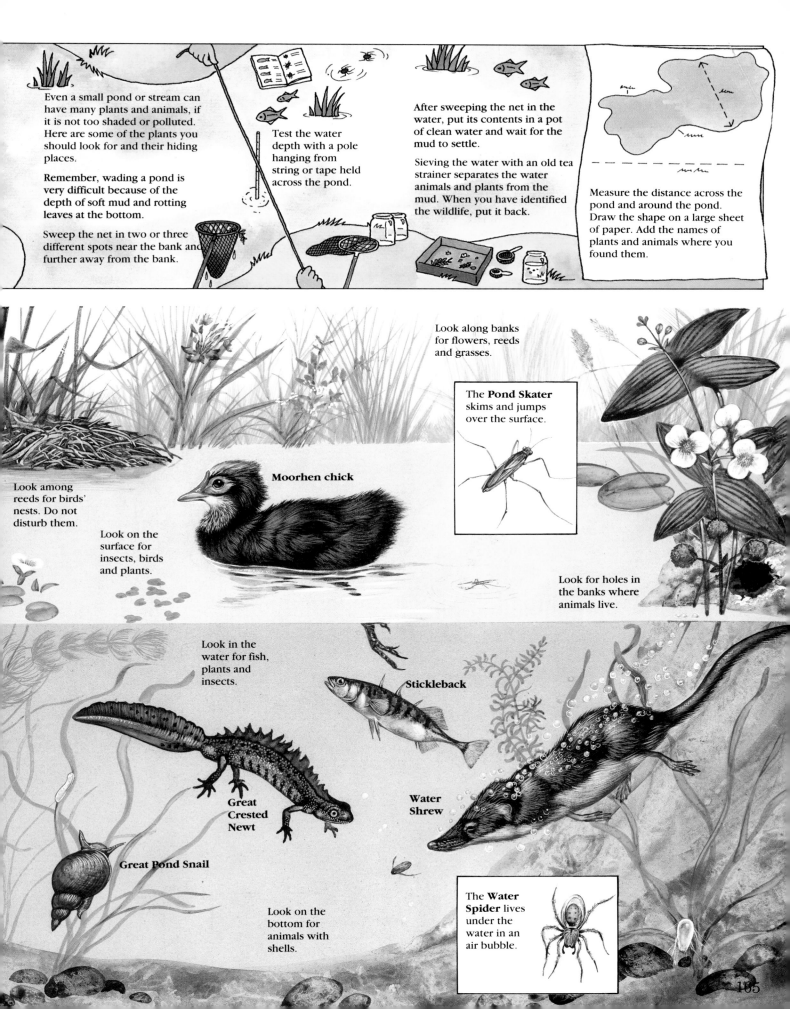

105

Living together

In a thriving pond there is a balance of different kinds of animals and plants, so that there is enough food for them all to survive. It is important not to disturb this balance.

How plants help

Animals need a gas called oxygen to survive. Water animals can get oxygen from the surface and some from the water itself. Oxygen in the water comes from the water plants.

Plants need sunlight to make food and produce their oxygen.

Canadian Pondweed

Try this experiment. Put some Canadian Pondweed in water and leave it in the sun. Oxygen bubbles will soon appear.

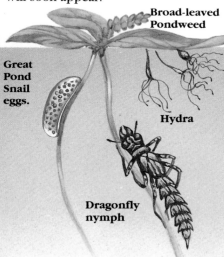

Broad-leaved Pondweed

Great Pond Snail eggs.

Hydra

Dragonfly nymph

Plants can provide animals with shade and shelter from enemies. They act as a support for eggs, such as those of the Great Pond Snail. Some tiny animals cling on to plants, such as the Hydra, which catch prey swimming by. Insects, such as the Dragonfly, use plant stems to climb out of the water when they are ready to become adults.

Pond food chains

The process of big animals eating smaller animals, which in turn eat even smaller animals, is called a food chain. In the food chain here, the Heron is at the top and eats animals in the second link, such as Perch. Perch eat animals in the third link and so the chain progresses down to algae in the fifth link.

There are many more animals at the bottom of the chain than at the top. This is because animals at the bottom are small, and a larger animal needs to eat many of them to survive.

Each type of animal eats many different things, so a pond has many different food chains.

Plants, such as algae, are often at the bottom of a food chain.

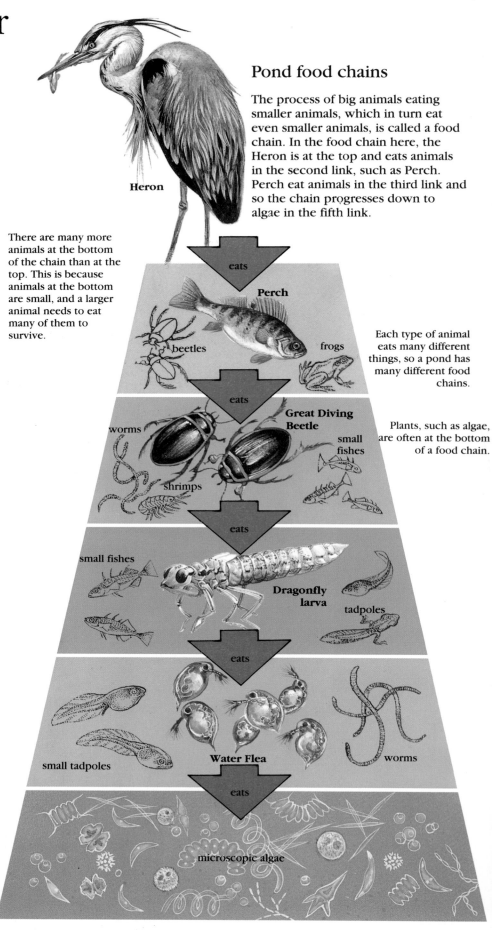

Heron

eats

Perch

beetles

frogs

eats

Great Diving Beetle

worms

shrimps

small fishes

eats

small fishes

Dragonfly larva

tadpoles

eats

small tadpoles

Water Flea

worms

eats

microscopic algae

Pollution

Human beings have a lot to answer for. Their pollution is a serious threat to the plants and animals living in the fresh water of rivers, ponds and streams. Here are some of the ways, not all man made though, that fresh water can become polluted. Phosphates from detergents in the home, such as those used to wash clothes, pass through sewage works and into fresh water. Phosphates cause water plants to grow strongly. When they die, the plants are broken up by bacteria which use up all the oxygen in the water. Water animals need oxygen to live, so this lack of oxygen can kill them. Human sewage entering rivers is also broken up by bacteria which starve the rivers of oxygen. Another problem from sewage is that it can cause fungus to grow which kills off plants.

The stream is usually clear and unpolluted at its source.

Mining waste floats on the surface, blocking out the light which plants need to make food. Some pieces of waste settle into spaces in the river bed where animals live.

Burning fossil fuels, such as petrol in cars and coal in power stations, releases sulphur and nitrogen into the air. These two gases make the rain more acid. This acid rain falls into fresh water and can kill fish.

Farmers use fertilizers on their land to grow more crops Some of these chemicals are washed off the land by rain into fresh water, or seep through the ground into fresh water. Fertilizers can make water plants grow faster and bigger. The more decaying plants there are, the less oxygen there is for water animals to breath. Algae grows faster and bigger too. This can cause the water to become murky and so cut off light from water plants growing at the bottom.

Poisons and chemical from factories are released into rivers. These can kill fish and make the water smell bad.

Water sports, such as boating and water skiing can disturb animal and plant life and damage river banks.

Overhanging tress block out the light from water plants and stop them growing. Fallen leaves from the trees use up much oxygen as they rot by the activity of bacteria. This is not a man made problem, but it can be solved by humans cutting back the trees.

Rain running off large heaps of manure can poison fish.

Rubbish dumped into ponds poisons the water and kills pond life. Water birds can get trapped by rubbish, such as string and wire, and die.

Kingfishers

Female

Male

Mallards

Male

Female

Female

Pochards

Male

During courtship, some male birds, such as the Kingfisher, offer the females a present of food. When the female has accepted her present, this means she is ready to mate.

The Mallard is a common duck, so you have a very good chance of seeing the male's striking courtship display. He dives, flaps his wings, sprays water from his bill, whistles and grunts. The female

attracts the male by jerking her head backwards and forwards. The male Pochard swims around the female and jerks his head backwards and forwards to attract her.

Looking after the young

Grey Herons

Some birds, such as the Grey Heron, are born helpless. They are blind, have no feathers, and cannot leave the nest for over a month. The young beg for food by pecking at their parents' bills.

Other types of young bird beg for food with loud cries or gaping beaks. Some birds, such as ducks and grebes, have feathers and can swim and feed a few hours after hatching.

Keeping the young safe

Little Grebes (or **Dabchicks**)

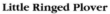

Little Grebe chicks can swim soon after they hatch. Sometimes they climb on to their parents' backs to keep safe from danger.

Little Ringed Plover

Like many birds that nest on the ground, the Little Ringed Plover moves away from the nest pretending to be hurt to divert an enemy from its young and eggs.

Watching water insects

When you visit a pond or stream, you will soon spot several different types of insects. Look in the air, on the water's surface and in the water itself. To help you to identify an insect, note down its colour, the shape and number of its wings, where you saw it, and any other details.

All adult insects have bodies with three parts, three pairs of legs, and usually a pair of antennae or feelers. Many have wings at some time in their lives.

Most insects breathe by taking in air through holes in their bodies. Many underwater insects carry a bubble of air on their bodies, which they collect at the surface.

A thin film on the water's surface stops an insect from sinking. See how this works by floating a needle on water.

Place some blotting paper on the surface of some water. Now place a needle on the blotting paper.

Watch the needle stay on the surface as the blotting paper soaks up water and sinks.

The **Water Boatman** swims and takes in air at the surface, upside down. It has a sharp bite when picked up.

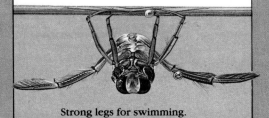
Strong legs for swimming.

Above the water

A **Damselfly** at rest holds its wings together.

Swarms of **Mayflies** rise and fall over the water.

Dragonflies fly in pairs when mating.

A **Mayfly** has two or three long threads at the end of its body.

Look for these flying insects in spring and early summer, when they emerge from the pupa or nymph. Most stay close to the water, and they all breed there.

On the surface

The **Water Measurer** moves slowly. The hairs on its body stop it from getting wet.

Tiny **Springtails** can jump 30 cm, using their hinged tails.

The **Pond Skater** slides rapidly over the surface. It can also jump.

Whirligig Beetles have one pair of eyes looking into the water, and another pair looking into the air. They whirl and spin while hunting for food.

Notice the different ways that these insects move on the water's surface. They feed mostly on dead insects that fall on the water.

Under the water

Breathing tube

The **Water Scorpion** is not a real scorpion at all. It takes in air at the surface through a breathing tube. It stores air under its wing cases.

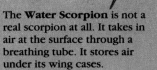

The antenna breaks the surface film of the water while it collects air.

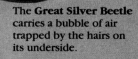
Air bubble

The **Great Silver Beetle** carries a bubble of air trapped by the hairs on its underside.

How insects feed

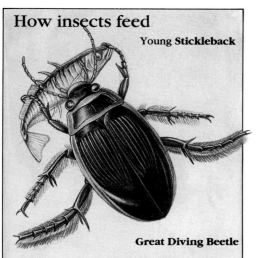

Young Stickleback

Great Diving Beetle

Many water beetles eat other animals. The Great Diving Beetle feeds on tadpoles, insects and small fish. Its prey can sometimes be larger than itself.

The front legs are used for catching prey.

Tadpole

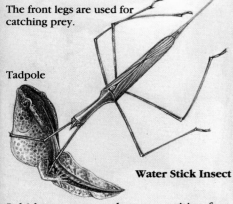

Water Stick Insect

It hides among reed stems, waiting for prey. The front legs shoot out to catch animals, such as insects and tadpoles. Then it sucks out their juices.

The Lesser Water Boatman feeds on algae and rotting plants on the bottom. Unlike the Water Boatman, it swims with its right side up.

Lesser Water Boatman

Making an insect aquarium

This picture shows the things you will need to make an aquarium. Keep the aquarium near a window, but not in direct sunlight. If you use tap water, add some pond water and leave it for a few days before adding the animals. Do not fill it too deep and add snails to keep the sides from being covered in algae.

Nymphs and larvae

Feed nymphs and larvae on worms or tiny bits of raw meat. Remove uneaten pieces of meat or the water will become unpleasant.

Clean waterproof tank. (A plastic or glass bowl will do.)

Pond or tap water.

Twig for nymphs to climb on to.

Stones

Snail

Washed sand or gravel 5 cm deep.

Flying insects

To keep flying insects, such as beetles, put a lid or some fine netting over the aquarium to stop them from escaping.

Glass or plastic cover resting on small pieces of wood.

Leave a gap for air to get in.

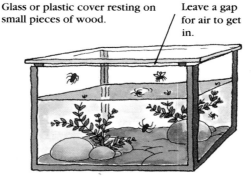

Feed beetles on worms or tiny bits of raw meat.

Tiny insects

Keep these insects in separate containers, or they will eat each other. Feed them on pieces of meat or worms.

Margarine pot

Clear plastic cover with air holes.

Lid with air holes.

Rubber band

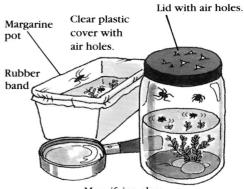

Magnifying glass

Fierce insects

Keep tiny insects in a jar or pot. Put in pond water, some mud and a few plants. Do not forget to make air holes in the clear plastic cover or the jar's lid.

Great Diving Beetle

Water Stick Insect

Water Scorpion

Water Boatman

Remember!

Only take a few insects from the water. Make sure they have the right food and enough room. Always return them to the pond or stream when you have finished studying them.

177

How insects grow

You can find some exciting insects in ponds and streams, even in polluted water. Most insects go through several stages of development from the egg to adult. (Follow the life cycle of the Caddis Fly in this section.) The early stages may last for years, but the adult may only live for a few hours or days.

Some water insects, such as water beetles, spend all their lives in the water. Others, such as the Alder Fly, leave the water when fully grown.

The Caddis Fly

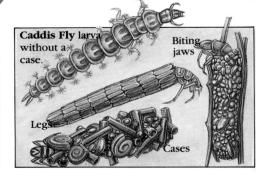

Eggs in jelly.

Egg

The Caddis Fly begins its life in fresh water. The eggs are laid in jelly on plants or stones, either above or below the water's surface.

Caddis Fly larva without a case.

Biting jaws

Legs

Cases

Larva

The larva hatches from the egg. Then it may make a protective case of shells, stones or leaves. The larva eats plants from the bottom of the pond.

Where insects lay eggs

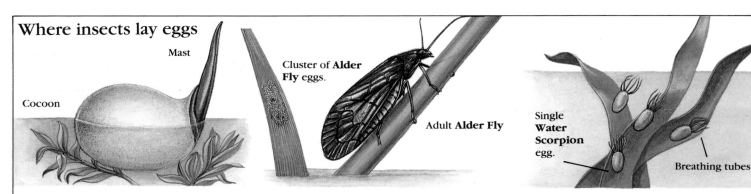

Mast

Cocoon

Cluster of **Alder Fly** eggs.

Adult **Alder Fly**

Single **Water Scorpion** egg.

Breathing tubes

On the water

The Great Silver Beetle lays its eggs in a silky cocoon on the surface of the water. The hollow "mast" of the cocoon allows air to reach the eggs.

Above the water

Look for insect eggs on water plants and stones above the water's surface. When the larvae hatch, they fall or crawl down into the water.

Below the water

Some insects lay their eggs under the water on plants or stones, or on the mud bottom. The Water Scorpion lays its eggs on plant stems.

Larvae and nymphs

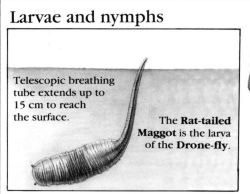

Telescopic breathing tube extends up to 15 cm to reach the surface.

The **Rat-tailed Maggot** is the larva of the **Drone-fly**.

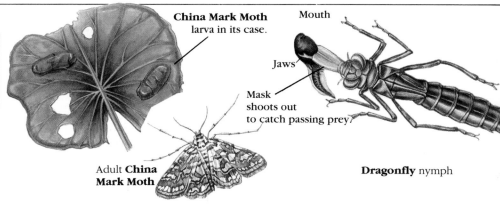

China Mark Moth larva in its case.

Mouth

Jaws

Mask shoots out to catch passing prey.

Adult **China Mark Moth**

Dragonfly nymph

Put some mud from a pond or stream into a dish. Add a little water and sieve it with an old tea strainer. See if you can spot the Rat-tailed Maggot and its breathing tube.

Look for small holes in the leaves of Water Lilies and Pondweed. Underneath the leaves, you may see this moth larva, which makes a case out of the leaves and also feeds on them.

A young dragonfly is called a nymph when it hatches from the egg. It has a strong pair of jaws fixed to a hinge, called a mask. See how the adult emerges from the nymph on page 19.

Birds

Measurements are from beak to tip of tail.

Grey Heron. Nests in trees. Feeds in shallow water and marshes. 90 cm.

Coot. Lives in flocks outside breeding season. Notice white mark on head. 38 cm.

Chick

Snipe. Hides among plants near water, where it feeds. Long bill for probing in mud. 27 cm.

Spotted Crake. White spotted body. Feeds at water edge at dusk. Very secretive. 23 cm.

Osprey. Dives to catch fish in claws. Rare. A few breed in Scotland. 51-58 cm.

Great Crested Grebe. In lakes and reservoirs. Winters also on coast. 48 cm.

Winter

Summer

Chick

Moorhen. Common in parks. Notice white flash under tail. 33 cm.

Water Rail. Hides in reed beds. 28 cm.

Female

Male

Mallard. Most common duck. Often in parks. 58 cm.

Chick

Female

Male

Teal. Europe's smallest duck. 35 cm.

Summer

Winter

Black-headed Gull. Loses dark cap in winter. 35-38 cm.

Swallow. Summer visitor. Catches insects on the wing. 19 cm.

Yellow Wagtail. Lives in Britain. Blue-headed Wagtail in Central Europe. Other varieties in Europe (see below). 16.5 cm.

Yellow Wagtail

Pied wagtail

Female

Male

White Wagtail

Blue headed wagtail

Scandinavia

Italy

Spain and France

Grey Wagtail. Lives near fast-flowing streams. 18 cm.

White Wagtail. Lives in Europe. Pied Wagtail in Britain. 18 cm.

Reed Bunting. By rivers and in marshy places. 15 cm.

If you cannot see the bird you want to identify here, turn to the pages earlier in the book on birds, and you may be able to see a picture of it there.

Index

Illustrated by: Mike Atkinson, Dave Ashby, Graham Austin, John Barber, Amanda Barlow, David Baxter, Andrew Beckett, Joyce Bee, Stephen Bennett, Roland Berry, Isabel Bowring, Hilary Burn, Liz Butler, Lynn Chadwick, Patrick Cox, Christine Darter, Michelle Emblem, Don Forrest, John Francis, Victoria Gordon, Edwina Hannam, Tim Hayward, Christine Howes, Chris Howell-Jones, David Hurrell, Ian Jackson, Roger Kent, Colin King, Deborah King, Jonathan Langley, Richard Lewington, Ken Lilly, Josephine Martin, Malcolm Mcgregor, Doreen McGuinness, Richard Millington, Robert Morton, David Nash, Barbara Nicholson, David Palmer, Julie Piper, Gillian Platt (The Garden Studio), Charles Raymond (Virgil Pomfret Agency), Barry Raynor, Phillip Richardson, Jim Robins, Michèlle Ross, Gwen Simpson, Annabel Spenceley, Peter Stebbing, Joyce Tuhill, David Watson, Phil Weare, Adrian Williams, Roy Wiltshire, John Yates